THE
POLYTUNNEL
HANDBOOK

The
Polytunnel
Handbook

Andy McKee & Mark Gatter

green books

First published in 2009
by Green Books Ltd
Foxhole, Dartington,
Totnes, Devon TQ9 6EB

Reprinted 2009

Printed in the UK on Corona Natural 100% recycled paper
by TJ International Ltd

ISBN 978 1 900322 45 4

Contents

Acknowledgements

To Andy's parents, who encouraged even the doomed egg-plant experiment.

To Mark's family, who, despite everything, still manage to look pleased to see him.

To Toni, for all her love, encouragement and vats of tea.

To Linda, without whom a garden would be just another bit of land.

To Pat Bowcock, for allowing us to visit her formidable and inspiring tunnel, and for not losing Toni's hat.

To Amanda Cuthbert and all at Green Books, for being gentle with us.

To Frances Kelly, for not being gentle with us.

To Sean Barker of First Tunnels, James Gish, Vernon Griffiths, Rebecca Hillman, Diana Johnson, Carol Mulraney, El Parcels, Alan Roberts and Hugh Steinmann for their helpful responses to our endless questions.

Introduction

Walking into a polytunnel on a sunny day in March is like walking into a bubble of summer. Quiet and warm on even the coldest and rainiest day, it makes the perfect spot to retreat to with a gardening book when the drizzle gets you down. The plants outside may be battered by squalls and wilted by frost, but inside the tunnel the growing season is well under way. The new potatoes, planted in February, are already up – and there are carrots, radishes, lettuce, spinach, rocket, mizuna and many others just waiting to be picked.

The last decade has seen a huge increase in demand for organically produced vegetables. At the same time, local authorities are struggling to cope with unprecedented demand for allotments, with a record 100,000 people on the waiting list nationally at the time of writing. Clearly, something interesting and fundamental is happening to the way we think about our food – and with several television series capitalizing on the trend, 'growing your own' is quickly becoming fashionable.

More and more people are waking up to the idea that organic vegetables eaten straight from your own plot are not only fresher, tastier and more nutritious than shop-bought produce; they cost less, and have a lower carbon footprint too. But here in northern Europe we have a relatively short growing period and unreliable summers, so a little help is needed with some crops. Growing under cover extends the growing season by around a month at each end of the year, and makes growing your own food right through the year a more realistic proposition, even in the far north.

A greenhouse can offer many of the same benefits, but polytunnels are less expensive and so you can afford a larger one. This is not to say that tunnels have to be enormous; they come in all sizes, from multi-span hangars for professional growers right down to 1.8m x 2.4m (6' x 8') houses for smaller gardens. For a medium-sized structure you can expect to cover twice the area for half the price and – unlike greenhouses – the bigger they get, the better value they are. This means that tunnel gardeners need not be limited to a few tomato plants in grow-bags; from watermelons and sweet potatoes in summer to salad crops in the dead of winter, the protected environment of a polytunnel can be achieved without artificial heat or light.

How big a tunnel to get depends entirely on you, but you can always decide to add on an additional hoop or two at a later date to accommodate grander plans; more crops, a small patio, or a peach tree – whatever takes your fancy. Even if the size you choose now seems large compared to a little greenhouse, once you get used to growing throughout the year you will find that polytunnel space is like storage space in a kitchen – no matter how much you have, you could always use a little more.

Polytunnels usually need no planning permission and are simpler to erect than most flat-packed furniture. The frame lasts indefinitely, and while the polythene cover needs to be replaced every five years, a replacement generally costs less than 20% of the original outlay. The old cover is recyclable, being made of the same material as plastic bags. Although covers made from recycled or renewable plastics are not yet available, an equivalent area of greenhouse glass takes ten times as much energy to manufacture – but cannot reasonably be expected to last ten times as long, making polytunnels the greener option.

Andy says:

> "Within a year of putting up our first polytunnel, my family and I were growing 80% of the vegetables that we needed. The year after that we had started to get the hang of polytunnel growing, and that figure rose to 95% – and we were selling surplus produce at the gate to pay for chicken-feed and general supplies. If I had to give up one garden tool it certainly wouldn't be the tunnel – I'd sooner part with my spade!"

Mark says:

> "Living on heavy clay in the rain shadow of the Brecon Beacons isn't really a recipe for gardening success – but with our polytunnel we are guaranteed fresh greens right through the year, as well as some un-dreamed-of luxuries: organic globe artichokes in January, for example. We've already decided where we're going to put an even bigger tunnel next year."

Chapter 1

Planning your Purchase

A step-by-step guide from first thoughts to ordering

Having made the decision that polytunnel ownership is for you, the temptation is to rush off and order one straight away. Catering for customers who do exactly that, there are some friendly-looking sellers around who keep everything looking very simple and offer you a choice of only a few different kits. Don't be fooled; this simplicity is for their benefit, not for yours. At best you will miss out on some of the choices that make polytunnels such a flexible asset: at worst you will end up with a completely unsuitable product.

On the other hand, approaching a polytunnel manufacturer directly can leave you bewildered by the range of products and accessories on offer: different films, different ventilation strategies and a choice of door options, to name but a few. In reality these things are only confusing if you are not clear about exactly what you need from your polytunnel, and that's why there are a few things to consider before you're completely ready to go ahead.

Planning permission

The very first thing you need to think about is whether anything is likely to prevent you from putting a tunnel where you would like to put it. You should contact your local council's planning department to find out if you need planning permission. Despite controversy over larger commercial applications, at the time of writing single-span tunnels for domestic use don't need permission in most areas, but the position varies depending on where you live; in Andy's stamping ground in West Dorset, for example, you don't need permission unless the structure is concreted into place or connected to mains services. We would advise anyone who is told that they need permission to ask for a copy of the relevant guidance that the planning officers follow, since there is often confusion between the rules for domestic use and those for commercial growers.

There is also a layer of more local bureaucracy to consider before you go any further. If the polytunnel is on your own property, this just means checking to see whether there are any restrictions written into your deeds. This is unlikely to be a hindrance, but if you are considering erecting the tunnel on an allotment, then there will probably be specific rules that you will have to follow. While you need to be aware of what these rules say, don't speak to the allotments manager until you have a better idea of just what you would like to do. Nothing is more likely to produce a negative reaction than vagueness on your part.

Decisions on use

Now it's time to ask yourself a very simple question, but one that often goes unasked; what *exactly* do you want to use your tunnel for? This question will strike at the very heart of your installation. All subsequent questions – where the tunnel will be sited, what size it should be, whether water will be needed – hinge on what you intend your polytunnel to do. For example, if you intend to use it to bring on hanging baskets of flowers, then you will need easy access to water, a decent potting bench, and perhaps some extra insulation and/or heat for very cold conditions. On the other hand, if you just want to shelter chickens in winter, then you need excellent ventilation and room outside one end to give the birds a netted run. Incidentally, polythene-covered tunnels are not suitable for livestock in summer; for that, you need a shade house (see p.14).

Make a list of all the uses you have in mind for your tunnel, and have a stab at listing the characteristics you think will be needed for each. At this point it is essential to read some of the later chapters first, particularly the sections on irrigation (pp.53-6) and ventilation (pp.58-9), and then come back to your list again. You might be surprised at what you find, and save yourself a lot of heartache into the bargain.

How big, and where?

Moving from the general to the highly specific, size and site questions have to be decided on together. There's no point in opting for a 48'-long tunnel if it means running it diagonally across the back garden, and likewise there's no mileage in identifying a nice spot hidden behind a hedge if it means getting a tunnel that's too narrow for the big beds you've got planned. So, with size *and* site in mind, here are a few things to think about.

Sun

Unheated polytunnels stay warm inside by trapping solar energy (the aptly-named 'greenhouse effect'), so it's absolutely essential that the tunnel receives good light. This is particularly important in the morning to get the interior temperature up quickly after the cool of the night, so ensure that there is no dense shading directly to the east of the proposed site. If you want to make the most of the sun, then orient the ridge-pole of the tunnel as close to east-west as you can, whereas if you don't want things to get too hot in summer you might swing more towards north-south, or place your tunnel a little way to the north of a deciduous tree which can provide some shade in summer only. However, don't site your tunnel beneath overhanging branches, or you run the risk of leaves and other debris falling on to the film.

Wind

Take a good look at any polytunnels in your area; if they all face in the same direction then it may be to provide some protection from strong prevailing winds. Tunnels will resist wind better if it strikes them broadside on, even though the profile offered to the wind is larger, since the most vulnerable part of the structure is around the doors. Polytunnels are immensely strong if they are installed correctly, but never underestimate the power of a winter storm. Try to make sure that your site is sheltered from the prevailing winds, and if that means planting a windbreak, you might wish to consider this now, while you are still at the planning stage.

Location

Although polytunnels can be mounted on gentle slopes, there are drawbacks to doing this. A gradient running end-to-end can be coped with, although the doors will have to open onto the downhill side unless you are prepared to do some digging to accommodate them. Slopes running from side to side, however, cause more serious problems since each pair of ground tubes which anchor the structure to the ground have to be exactly level. For best results and least work, the site should be as level as possible. Don't underestimate the work involved in levelling even a fairly small area by hand; if possible, work with what you've got.

Mark says:

> "My tunnel is on a slight end-to-end slope and it's not a problem – in fact, given the heavy clay soil here, it's an advantage. If the tunnel was on level ground, there'd be nowhere for runoff to go."

Another factor to consider is the fertility of the site's soil (although raised beds are a possibility if the soil is poor) and how well it drains, since the runoff to either side in a downpour is very considerable. Hollows and patches that are already damp are a poor idea. Finally, beware of putting the tunnel in a frost pocket – any spot in which frost lingers on a cold morning is to be avoided.

Clearance

When you are considering what size the 'footprint' of the tunnel is, allow at least 1m (3') spare on all sides. In this way, a 4.25m x 5.5m (14' x 18') tunnel ideally needs a footprint of 6m x 7.25m (20' x 24'). Not only will you need this space when you put the film on the frame, but you will need to keep it clear of tall growth if you are to avoid damage and low-level shading.

Water

At the very least, it's essential to have a standpipe or substantial water storage near your polytunnel (see 'Water in the Tunnel' on pp.52-8). Even with the best water management, the bigger the tunnel the more water it will use – so make things easy on yourself. Remember that if this means laying a water-pipe to supply a new tap you will need to bury it deeply enough to avoid frost damage. Your water company will be able to offer you advice on how deep this should be, but this advice may not be terribly practical. As an alternative, ask some local gardeners, or else drain the system for the winter. The closer you can site your tunnel to an existing water supply the better.

Power

By the same token, running an electricity supply to your tunnel does not come cheap. However, relatively few things in the tunnel are likely to need power, and most needs can be met by using battery or solar power instead. Adding mains power may also require planning permission, so think carefully about whether you really need electricity.

Visibility

Thanks to some well-publicised opposition to large-scale agricultural operations, the appearance of polytunnels is sometimes the source of contention. The visual impact can often be softened with screening plants, but take the time to consider where the tunnel could be placed to minimize its impact. Do remember that your neighbours may be looking at the structure too, and might well appreciate your taking the time to look at the plot from their side of the fence. Another visibility factor to consider is security; although it's not something anyone likes to think about, an inconspicuous tunnel is less likely to draw attention from thieves and vandals.

Zoning

In permaculture terms, a polytunnel falls into Zone One. In simple terms, this means that it needs frequent visits during the day; even if you do nothing else, you will need to open the doors in the morning, close them at night, and pop in once or twice to check on plants or do a spot of watering. There are other options for watering if your polytunnel is not on the same site as your home, but it should normally be placed as close to the house as other factors allow. At the very least there should be a good path to get you there and back without any spills on soggy winter mornings.

Convenient access to your tunnel is a big plus – especially when you're in the middle of cooking dinner and remember that you should have picked some basil earlier. For more information on zoning, see *Permaculture Two* by Bill Mollison (detailed in *Appendix 2: Further Reading*).

The tunnel's own effects

Do not forget that the tunnel itself will affect the microclimate around it. To the north side there will be some shading, particularly in winter; to the south there will be some extra reflected light which may benefit sun-loving plants. The tunnel will act as a partial windbreak on the leeward side, but putting it near other structures may well result in a funnelling effect as the wind is forced between them – and this is something to ignore at your

Probably the most significant effect, however, will be that the ground to both sides of the tunnel will become damper than before due to run-off. Depending on the slope and soil type of your site this may become a problem during wet weather, in which case you may need to take steps to improve drainage, such as laying a section of land drain to carry the water away. As an alternative, use the run-off to your advantage by attaching flexible gutters to the cover so that some of the rainfall can be stored for future use (this is detailed on p.24).

Polytunnel types

Before going on to make a final decision about the size of your tunnel, you need to consider what sort of structure to buy.

Polytunnel

A basic polytunnel is a simple single-span structure made from hoops supporting a polythene film. This creates a bubble of still air which is quickly warmed by solar energy, creating a warm micro-climate; basically, it is a walk-in cloche. Compared with a greenhouse it is more difficult to keep frost-free in winter and needs additional insulation if it is to be heated. Due to diffusion of light by the film, propagation is slower than in a greenhouse in the spring but by the same token leaf scorch is less of a problem in summer.

The Greenhouse Effect

Polytunnels come in a wide range of widths and styles, and there are many additional options to choose from, making them extremely versatile for general use. Older models have curved sides, leading to a certain amount of wasted space, and unless your tunnel is very wide it is well worth paying a little extra for straighter side sections. Polytunnel covers typically last five years before becoming brittle, with light transmission falling a little each year. They are easy to replace and recycle, however, and cost only a fraction of the original tunnel price.

Flat-ended tunnels

By using a separate sheet of polythene for each gable end, flat-ended tunnels such as the 'Harlow' avoid the need to pleat the cover around the door frame and are fitted with sliding doors, rather than hinged ones. Gable ends of this type are only available in widths up to 3m, and while they can be covered in tinted polythene and provide an overall appearance which is neater than that of a regular tunnel, they are more expensive and confer few practical advantages.

Shade houses

Shade houses (also known as airflow houses) are a variation of the polytunnel where the polythene cover is replaced by shade netting. This cuts down sunlight by around 50% and allows gentle airflow through the tunnel at all times. Sometimes a high side rail is used to allow a section of polythene to act as a 'roof' on top, giving some shelter in wet conditions. Shade houses are used for some specific applications including hardening off championship vegetables, providing shelter for livestock, and for growing shade-loving or temperature-sensitive plants such as chrysanthemums or orchids. Since only the covers are different, costs are similar to those of polytunnels.

Solar tunnels

A more sophisticated version of the polytunnel is the solar tunnel, which in terms of price and performance falls in the middle between standard polytunnels and the much more expensive Keder house. Solar tunnels have covers made from PVC with an embedded green mesh, giving a softer appearance and a longer life than a polytunnel cover – typically seven years to the polytunnel's five. The covers are supplied in sections with welded loops through which the tunnel-frame sections are passed, making them fit tightly and giving an easier installation than a standard tunnel.

This modular design confers one big advantage, which is that an additional section can be added at a later date without re-covering the whole tunnel. Solar tunnels are held down by screw-in anchor bolts, so it is possible to unscrew them from the ground and carry the whole thing to another site. However, on windy sites it is advisable to concrete the bolts into the ground, in which case the advantage of the screw-in anchor bolts is lost. The covers are easy to repair should a rip happen, and insulate slightly better than a plain PVC film. Solar tunnels are straight-sided and available in widths of 3m (9' 10") and 4.2m (13' 9"). There are also wider models with curved sides.

Keder houses

Keder houses are the Rolls-Royce of polytunnels, and are usually professionally assembled. Fabricated from a sandwich of bubbles between rigid plastic sheets, the structures will support several feet of snow without cracking (they are said to be strong enough to jump up and down on). They are guaranteed for ten years, and typically last about fifteen. Keder houses combine the advantages of both greenhouse and polytunnel, being straight-sided, very well insulated and practically airtight when closed – a real boon on freezing winter nights. They are available in widths of 2m (6' 6"), 3m (9' 10") and 4m (13'), the last size being a more serious piece of work with guttering and sidewall ventilation as standard. The most serious drawback is price of course, as they cost around five times as much as a typical polytunnel.

The biggest single advantage that the more sophisticated structures offer you is improved insulation, but this comes at a price. It is, however, possible to further insulate and heat areas within a standard polytunnel, so unless insulation comes high on your list of priorities or unless cost is not a major concern, it may well be that an ordinary polytunnel will be your best option. This is a decision you should take now because it affects the range of widths available to you, which in turn determines your internal layout. Once again, it is worth remembering that unless you choose a straight-sided option (offered by all manufacturers but not by all retailers) there will be a certain amount of space at the sides that is less useful because of the lack of clearance, the curvature of the cover leaving room for only quite low-growing plants.

Layout

At this stage it's worth thinking about what sort of internal layout you want to use, in case this means a change to the width of tunnel you have in mind.

To a certain extent the layout of domestic tunnels is dictated by their width. Given that most people have a maximum reach of about 60cm (2') from a path, and that paths should ideally be around (2') wide to allow you to kneel comfortably, there are only so many layouts that are feasible in an ordinary-sized tunnel.

The sample layouts below will give you some idea of what we mean by that, but you may have other ideas: one large and highly-productive tunnel we visited had haphazard triangular raised beds with a wood-shaving path meandering through them all, and very pleasant it was in there too. The choice of whether or not to use raised beds is dealt with in a later chapter (pp.48-51); this is something you should try to decide before your tunnel arrives, as preparatory digging is much easier to do before it goes up.

Finally, if you are placing some staging in your tunnel for potting and watering, don't forget to leave room for it. To get the full benefits of poly-tunnel growing we recommend a tunnel width of at least 3m (9' 10") with straight sides, or 4.2m (13' 9") without straight sides, and a ridge height of no less than 2.1m (7').

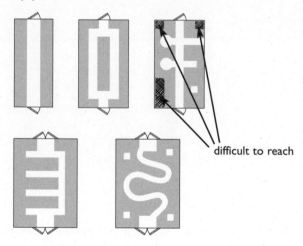

difficult to reach

Tunnel layouts

Convincing the neighbours

The last potential source of friction is from your neighbours (or your allotment manager, if you're thinking of putting a tunnel on your allotment). Consider how they might react. By now you should have a good idea of what you intend to do, enabling you to approach the discussion positively. After all, this is all about enhancing your environment, and the prospect of the occasional melon or out-of-season lettuce might well work wonders.

In the case of literal neighbours, you might be surprised by some of the strange ideas that people have about polytunnels. One group of neighbours that we heard about was worried about visual intrusion (which was a valid concern) and noise (which was not). To this day no-one knows exactly what sound they thought that tunnels made, but perhaps it's better not to ask. Be aware that in the minds of some people, the word 'polytunnel' conjures up images of the sort of poorly-covered algae-encrusted eyesore that you sometimes see cowering in the corner of a field, but in truth these are the abandoned barns of the polytunnel world.

Where to buy

With most goods, the old adage that "you gets what you pays for" holds true, and polytunnels are no exception. In the marketplace it's a general truism that purchasing direct from the manufacturers is the most cost-effective way to buy, but there are also retailers bringing tunnels into the UK from Europe and the rest of the world, sometimes surprisingly cheaply. However, you should be aware that not all polytunnels are created equal, and lightweight or poorly-constructed frames (the best ones are galvanised steel) are unlikely to last in the way that you had hoped. Likewise, a thin or poorly-specified cover will not perform so well nor last so long as a quality alternative, and the time and expense involved in replacing it more often is likely to make it a false economy. Make sure you buy UV-stabilised covers with a manufacturer's guarantee of at least four years.

If you are in a really exposed site or expecting a lot of snow, bear in mind that the thickness of the steelwork is not the only thing that gives a tunnel its strength. The distance between the hoops is also important, so you might consider reducing this. The addition of crop bars (a highly useful accessory in any case) can also help with snow loading. Another strength factor to consider is that in a 'trenched' installation, the frame is pulled downwards by the cover, which is held in place by the weight of soil used to bury the edges. If you opt for a model where the cover is clamped onto a base rail instead of being trenched, this downward force is lost and so you should concrete the frame into the ground or use an alternative way of fixing it such as anchor plates (see pp.19-20).

In *Appendix 1* you will find a list of suppliers. Take some time to look at what they have to offer, and ask for catalogues from any that look promising; sometimes a catalogue gives a fuller account of the range of goods that a company sells, particularly when it comes to accessories. It also pays dividends to ask for a copy of the installation instructions for the type of tunnel you want, since the quality of these varies hugely between suppliers.

Although putting a tunnel up is not complicated, it can seem so if you have never done it before, so read the instructions in advance and keep an eye out for problems such as contradictions and missing steps. If you have bought direct from a manufacturer, they are usually only too happy to answer telephone queries as you go along, but that will not help if you hit a snag while trying to attach a cover early on a Saturday morning. If you decide not to buy from a supplier because their instructions are poor, tell them so.

One other option that deserves a mention is buying second-hand. One of the beauties of polytunnels is the durability of the frame, but even so, careless handling can damage things. As with everything else, examine everything carefully as soon as you can. It may also be worth posting to your local Freecycle group (http://uk.freecycle.org) to see if anyone has unused staging or other such items. Freecycle is a web-based network that allows people to give (and get) things for free, and if you have never come across it before, it is well worth a look.

Cover options

Most manufacturers offer several different types of polythene cover, but beyond making sure that there is a satisfactory guarantee, do not fall into the trap of thinking that more expensive ones are automatically better. In fact, the most expensive types of film are those used for specific growing applications, such as dwarfing plants – not something you want to do by accident. There are several different brand names in use, so look at the product specification to see which features are being offered and how well they are claimed to work.

Clear polythene

Typically allows 95% light transmission. The name is something of a misnomer since the film has an opacifier to scatter the light; this reduces the problem of leaf-scorching (which means you can water in full sun if needs be) and reduces shading from neighbouring plants. Clear poly is suitable for typical spring-to-autumn growing, provided that you do not intend to heat the tunnel in winter.

'Smart Blue' polythene

This is a useful tool for professional growers because it produces small, bushy plants with enhanced leaf colour and a cooler summer environment. It is typically used for producing bedding plants, allowing for a longer sale period, but is not suitable for general use.

'Smart Green' polythene

This absorbs more light at the red end of the spectrum. Do not make the mistake of buying this film just because it will visually blend in better with the rest of the garden, as it is specifically designed to provide a cooler environment that is more suitable for shade-loving plants.

Thermal heat block (THB) polythene

Thermal heat block polythene contains thermal additives to reflect infra-red radiation, making the film retain heat better; if you are providing heat, this option can reduce energy costs considerably. THB film is used for any application where heat is important, such as propagation and overwintering vegetables. This type of cover is often given an anti-fog coating to reduce condensation, another risk factor for fungal diseases.

UVA and UVB filtered polythene

This reduces the risk of many fungal infections and decreases the activity of flying insects, which see in ultraviolet. It reduces the damage caused by aphids, and although it also reduces insect pollination, this is unlikely to be significant for the home grower (see 'Make your cover work for you' in *Preventing Pests*, pp.87-8).

Accessories

The word 'accessories' somehow implies that these are optional extras, but some of them (anti-hotspot tape, for example) are absolutely essential. The range of accessories varies hugely from one seller to another, and they are usually sold at reasonable prices.

Anchor plates

Anchor plates are a more recent innovation and, although not offered by all manufacturers, provide an alternative to concreting a frame into place. They are essentially flat plates through which the ground tubes pass. The ground tubes are fixed firmly to them using clamps, and then the anchor plates are buried in the soil, preventing the wind from moving the ground tubes.

Anchoring the structure in place with concrete or anchor plates is a good idea for installations with base rails, and for trenched tunnels in very windy areas. Anchor plates are easier and cheaper than concrete, and because they are not permanent, have no implications for planning permission.

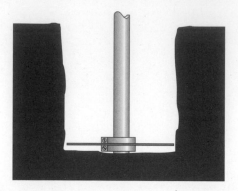

Anchor plate

Anti-hotspot tape

Anti-hotspot tape (confusingly also known as 'hotspot tape') is a vital part of your installation and is supplied as standard by most retailers as part of any kit; however, they can be a bit miserly about how much they give you. It is designed to cushion the film where it makes contact with the frame, thereby reducing the friction that will ultimately be the death of the cover. Manufacturers estimate that using anti-hotspot tape increases the lifetime of a cover by around a year, making it an excellent investment.

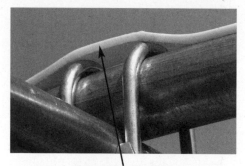

Anti-hotspot tape

Base plates

These bolt straight onto a hard surface, and are used instead of ground tubes when a tunnel is erected on a hard surface.

Base rails

These are used whenever a tunnel is being installed onto brick or concrete, or if the buyer has some reason not to want to dig a trench. Base rails are usually timber affairs held onto the frame with special fittings, and the cover is pulled round them and then secured. More sophisticated 'grab rails' are also available. Base rails allow for easy tightening of the cover, even after the tunnel has been standing for a while, but make it essential to secure the tunnel frame by concreting in the ground tubes or by using anchor plates (see pp.19-20). You should give this serious thought, and check for any local planning implications. However, using the 'grab' type of base rails still allows you to bury the edges of the film in a shallow trench to prevent draughts.

Manufacturers say:

> "The trench vs. base rail dilemma is one that we wish customers would consider more carefully before they order. Many people order a trenched kit, but end up placing a second order for a base rail accessory pack when they realise how much work digging the trench is going to be."

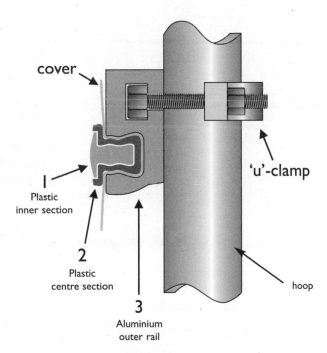

cover

'u'-clamp

I →
Plastic
inner section

2
Plastic
centre section

3
Aluminium
outer rail

hoop

Grab rail cross-section

Bubble film

This can be used to improve the insulation of a polytunnel if you are providing some artificial heat (see 'Heat' pp.59-63). It is thicker and stronger than the material commonly used when posting packages, and comes in wide rolls to minimise the number of joins.

Clamps

A few extra clamps can provide valuable attachment points, which are especially important if you are not fitting crop bars. Bear in mind that once the cover goes on it is impossible to fit any further clamps.

Crop bars

These run horizontally across from one side of the hoops to the other, typically at or just above a height of 1.8m (6'), and have diagonal braces for strength. They strengthen the hoops by around 20% in case of wind or heavy snow, but are also very handy for suspending hanging baskets and for securing plant supports. You cannot fit crop bars to the hoops at either end of your tunnel, so you will need two bars fewer than you have hoops.

Doors

Doors may not strike you as being an accessory, but some retailers treat them as such or supply you with only a single door at one end of the tunnel as standard. In a very small tunnel (3m / 10' or less) this may be adequate, but ideally you should have a door at either end. As the tunnel becomes longer, airflow becomes more important (see 'Ventilation' pp.58-9), so double doors at each end will provide better airflow. Most manufacturers will provide you with ready-made doors but a few will not, so if you are not confident about a little DIY joinery, this may be an issue.

Horticultural fleece

Horticultural fleece allows you to create a protected microclimate within the tunnel. In frost-prone areas this is a lifeline for less hardy plants.

Irrigation

Irrigation accessories can certainly be labour-saving, and the bigger the tunnel, the more time they will save (see 'Irrigation' pp.53-6).

Polythene repair tape

This is another must-have, preferably 10cm (4") wide. With the best will in the world it is only a matter of time before the end of a bamboo cane goes through your cover, or a trapped cat attempts to claw its way out, or some other nameless calamity occurs. The damage may be minor at the time, but the next gale to pass through your garden may well find its way into your tunnel, and what was a tiny hole quickly becomes a huge rip. Repair tape stops such minor damage from spreading.

Shade netting

This is an accessory that often appears without explanation in catalogues. It is a netting fabric, which is used instead of polythene when constructing a shade (or 'airflow') house (see p.14). It is *not* intended to be thrown over a polytunnel to reduce the amount of heat in high summer.

Side rails

These are similar to base rails, but they are fixed part way up the side of the tunnel. Attaching the polythene to a side rail rather than a base rail makes it possible to cover only the top of the frame with polythene. The sides of the tunnel can then be covered with netting, or with wooden slats if the tunnel is to be used for livestock.

Netting is used to improve airflow in large tunnels where ventilating using the doors at each end is not adequate (see 'Ventilation' pp.58-9), and becomes essential once the tunnel gets longer than around 9m (30') or if frequent visits to the tunnel are not possible. Of course this leaves the tunnel much more exposed to winter temperatures as well as gales, so some retailers offer wind-up polythene ventilation skirts to allow the gap to be closed easily at night.

A less expensive solution is to make a skirt yourself using extra film. This is simply an additional strip of polythene, edged top and bottom with wooden battens. The top batten is screwed to the existing side rail, and the lower one can be pegged to the ground when in use – or the skirt rolled up and tied to the side rail when it is not needed.

Staging

An area of staging is essential in any polytunnel, unless you are lucky enough to have an area of staging in a greenhouse. This is essentially a bench or table giving a working surface at a convenient height for pots and trays, and although this is unlikely to be free of ants, slugs and other pests, it can be made so by applying a little Vaseline or tree grease around the legs. This is highly recommended, as there are so many places for pests to hide on a potting bench that a single renegade slug can cause untold damage until you finally track it down.

Another option for staging is to suspend a wooden frame covered in sturdy mesh from the tunnel hoops or crop bars. Supported at each corner so that it does not rock, this type of bench is absolutely slug-proof and allows light through to plants beneath, and can easily be removed (or tied up out of the way) if it is no longer needed later in the season.

Most retailers offer staging options, either freestanding or fixed to the tunnel frame, but do make sure that the size is going to be suitable for you. Some commercial staging is worryingly low or shallow, which may save on materials but is no good at all for your back. As an alternative to staging you might consider getting hold of a small table from Freecycle (see p.18) and modifying it, or making your own.

Storm braces

These can be used to increase the strength of intermediate hoop joints. They bind the upper part of the hoop more firmly to the lower, preventing the joint from moving in a high wind, but are less important for installations without a base rail.

Tunnel gutter

This is a simple V-shaped piece of extruded plastic with an adhesive backing, which is applied to the wall of the tunnel, leaving the end over a barrel, bucket or down-pipe. The gutter is sufficiently flexible to pass over the frame hoops, and although the profile is too shallow to cope with heavy rainfall, this is a useful low-tech way to harvest at least some of the water falling on your tunnel and can fill a barrel surprisingly quickly.

Weed-control membrane

This is one way to keep your paths clear of weeds and grass, particularly if your tunnel has been erected on previously fertile lawn. However, to make sure you get a decent lifetime out of the membrane, you will need to mulch it with wood shavings, bark or similar material.

Waiting for your order

At last it is time to pick up the phone and place your order, and, barring surprises, you should then have an expected delivery date. There is plenty to do until then, not least preparing the polytunnel site and digging out any soil beds (see pp.48-50 for advice on bed types). If you have not already done so, this is also the time to get any windbreak planting done. You will need to arrange for some help on the day you cover your tunnel; four people are good, and six even better. However, putting the frame of the tunnel up and digging any trenching is likely to take some time, so make sure these tasks are done before your helpers arrive.

Chapter 2

The Big Day

Erecting the frame

The basic procedure for putting up a tunnel frame is more or less the same regardless of the manufacturer. To make the most of your helpers, have the frame assembled before they arrive. Putting a frame up is very quick if you have done it before, but if it is your first time with a particular set of instructions, it can be quite time-consuming; so, if it's something you are not familiar with, allow a full day for it.

It is, of course, vital to follow the manufacturer's instructions for your installation to the letter, but the following should give you some idea of what to expect. If the manufacturer's instructions are well written you should have no queries – but just in case, bear in mind there will be no one there to telephone at weekends.

Preparations

The very first thing to do when your tunnel kit arrives is to check off all the components against the supplier's invoice carefully, and to store the invoice and receipt in a safe place; you will need them again, even if it is only to find the size of the cover for replacement.

At the heart of any tunnel installation is the 3,4,5 triangle, otherwise known as Pythagoras' theorem. The idea that a triangle with sides of these ratios will give you a perfect right angle has been with us since ancient times, and you ignore it at your peril; you can buy the plushest tunnel kit and the best quality cover you like, but if you don't get your hoops exactly right, you won't get a tight fit and the cover will have a drastically reduced lifespan.

1. Begin by clearing the tunnel footprint of vegetation, including the 90cm (3') of clear space around it.

2. To set ground tubes using the 3,4,5 triangle, decide on the exact position of one side of the tunnel and put a corner tube at each end, measuring the distance carefully and putting the tubes no more than a few inches into the ground in case they have to be repositioned.

3. Now for the triangle. Run a string line between the two corner tubes and measure four metres (or four yards) along it from one of them, putting a marker stake into the ground at that point.

4. From the same corner, run the string line at an approximate right angle to the side. Measure three metres (or yards) from the corner, but do so using a mark on the string rather than a position on the ground. Then run a tape measure from the marker stake to the end of the string line, and reposition them both until you have a five-metre (or five-yard) diagonal meeting the three-metre mark (or three-yard mark) on the string line – at which point you will have an accurate right angle. Peg the string line down, measure along it to the correct width of your tunnel, and put a third corner tube in place at that point.

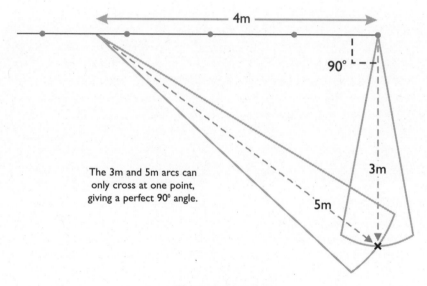

The 3m and 5m arcs can only cross at one point, giving a perfect 90° angle.

4m

90°

3m

5m

The 3, 4, 5 triangle

5. Repeat for the far end, then check your work by measuring the tunnel's two diagonals; if you have been accurate they should tally to within 5cm (2").

6. Once you are happy with the footprint, run the string line along each long side so that you can measure and position the intermediate tubes.

Setting the ground tubes / anchor plates

For a trenched installation, the weight of backfill on the cover itself anchors the tunnel structure to the ground. In this case, once you are happy with the position of the ground tubes you simply hammer them into the ground, using a spirit level to keep them absolutely vertical and a piece of timber to avoid damaging the end of the tubes with your hammer. If, however, you have opted for a base rail, then you will need to concrete the ground tubes in place, or hold them firmly with anchor plates. If you are fixing to a hard surface, then you will be using base plates instead of ground tubes; having marked your surface as described above, these are simply screwed or bolted onto the surface.

Anchor plates are very easy to install. Starting with one corner tube, remove it and dig out a hole 45cm (18") deep, and about the same wide. Attach a clamp *very tightly* near the foot of the tube and place it in the hole. Tap it into place, checking its position with the string line and tape measure. The anchor plate is then dropped onto the tube and held in place by a second clamp, after which the hole is backfilled. Continue checking the position of the tube during this process, as it can easily be moved as the earth around it is tamped down.

Concreting ground tubes into place is done in a similar manner, except the hole only needs to be 30cm (1') wide. The ground tubes are tapped into the bottom of the holes and their position checked, then hammered almost to ground level and the hole backfilled with a five-to-one mixture of aggregate and cement, stopping 5cm (2") below ground level and covering over with earth once the concrete has set. Only the corner tubes need to be concreted in. One word of warning: in some instances concreting ground tubes into place requires planning permission, so check with your local authority before taking this step.

In each of these cases the most important ground tubes to secure are the corner ones, and it is not generally necessary to anchor the intermediate hoops except in exposed locations or if the tunnel width exceeds 4.25m (14'). However, if you are working from a kit which includes enough anchor plates in any case, then you would be well advised to use them all.

The hoops

Tunnel hoops are commonly supplied in sections, and are much easier to move about this way. Using the supplied fittings, assemble the hoops and put them onto the ground tubes. Pay particular attention to which fittings have to be on the hoops before you do so, and on which side of the ridge-pole they have to end up, particularly for any optional features such as crop bars.

The ridge-pole

When the hoops first go up they will be quite flexible and prone to movement, but once the ridge-pole is put together and connected to the hoops, the entire structure gets a lot stronger. The ridge-pole fixes the distance between the tops of the hoops, spreading any force between them all.

Adding diagonal bracing

Diagonal braces create a triangular and therefore rigid shape when connected to a point a metre or so above ground level on a corner hoop to the base of its nearest neighbour. This stops the end hoops from flexing, and this rigidity is transmitted to all the other hoops through the ridge- pole.

Fitting crop bars

Crop bars (also known as trusses) are highly useful accessories for all but the lowest of tunnel structures. Fitted to any or all of the hoops apart from the end hoops, they increase the load capacity of the hoops by around 20% and provide invaluable hanging and attachment points for plants and supports without any risk to the cover.

Erecting the door frame

Door frames are attached to the end hoops at the top, and partially buried into the ground at the bottom. The ground needs to be tamped down well so that they are as stable as possible. If any of the supplied timber for the frame needs to be cut, make sure that a good wood preservative is painted over the cut ends prior to burying them below ground level, otherwise it will rot quite quickly.

Trenching or fitting a base rail

Depending on which method of securing the cover you have chosen, at this point you will either need to dig a 30cm x 30cm (1' x 1') trench around the tunnel footprint, or install a base rail onto the hoops at low level.

Covering the tunnel

To prevent friction and heat from damaging the cover where it touches the hoops, padded adhesive tape must be applied to all the areas of the frame that will contact the cover. The tape can also be used to cushion any rough areas that might conceivably damage the cover.

With a number of helpers, the cover is pulled over the tunnel frame and the edges either buried into the trench or fixed to the base rail as applicable. The cover is also fitted around the door frames. This is covered in more detail in *Self-build Tunnels*, pp.33-46, but take particular care that the pleating is done working outwards from the middle, folding the pleats so that there are no pockets inside the tunnel to collect condensation and dead insects.

Tightening the cover

Although careful covering of the tunnel frame ensures that there is no slack in the cover, commercial tunnels allow for the later application of tension to the film resulting in less movement and a longer cover life. In the case of a trenched installation, this is usually done by loosening the clamps which hold the hoops onto the ground tubes, and physically lifting the hoops to stretch the film. If you have chosen a base rail, then this is pushed downwards and refastened to tighten the film, and the hoops are not adjusted.

Fitting the doors

Whether you have opted to make the doors yourself or bought them pre-fabricated, now is the time to fit them along with catches and bolts and any other door furniture. A stake hammered into the ground as a doorstop will help to prevent accidental damage to the film and frame if the doors are caught by the wind. Finally, put the manufacturer's instructions away safely where they can be found if they are needed again in future years.

Irrigation from day one

It might seem odd to put watering in as part of installation, but from the moment the cover goes on the inside of a tunnel receives no moisture except what you give it. Add to that a high internal temperature and (hopefully) good ventilation, and you will see that without your intervention the beds inside the tunnel will take only a day or two to dry out to a dangerous extent – see the section on soil in *The Tunnel Environment* pp.47-63, for details.

Obviously enough, the soil conditions in your tunnel (as well as the thirst of your plants) will determine how often watering needs to take place. In sandy soil, which drains quickly, you will need to water regularly and often. In heavier clay soils, the water will be retained for much longer and watering requirements will be reduced accordingly.

Maintaining your tunnel

Re-tensioning the cover

For all their apparent fragility, tunnels are remarkably strong, stable structures and require very little in the way of maintenance. Nevertheless, over time some slack tends to creep into your cover each year – particularly during the tunnel's first summer – and you should do what you can to re-tighten it. The more movement there is in the cover, the shorter its life will be. Re-tightening depends on the type of installation you have chosen and where the slack appears, and thus can mean lifting the hoops on the ground tubes, lowering the base rail, or adjusting the battening around the doors.

Washing the cover

In damp conditions your tunnel cover will become coated with a thin layer of green algae. This occurs so slowly that you may not notice it for some time, but it can seriously reduce the amount of light that gets through the cover. For this reason you will need to clean the cover once or possibly twice a year; a clean in early spring is quite definitely a must.

Thankfully, cleaning a tunnel need not take long. A soft mop is ideal for a small 3m-wide (10') tunnel, but take care not to put too much pressure on a cover that is more than three years old. As the film ages it becomes brittle, and it is fairly easy to accidentally damage a cover that would otherwise last a couple more years before requiring replacement. For wider tunnels, you will need a willing helper, an old sheet, two short lengths of rope (or clothes-line or similar), two tennis balls (or something that size), a soft car-washing brush, a garden hose, and a bucket of a suitable detergent solution.

First, tie a length of rope securely at each end of the sheet. Don't make any holes in the sheet, as it will only tear. Instead, place a tennis ball near the end of the sheet and wrap the sheet end back around it, so that the ball is in a pouch of sheeting; then tie the rope around the neck of the pouch, so that the ball acts as an anchor to secure the rope.

Dip the sheet into your detergent solution. To prevent damage to the tunnel film, a mild detergent such as Citrox is needed. This is an organic cleanser which inactivates many fungal spores, retards algal growth, and more importantly is harmless to plants, breaking down harmlessly in the soil.

Using the hose, thoroughly wet the tunnel and throw the sheeting over it so that it hangs down on either side, as if it were an extra hoop. You and your helper now have to take turns to pull the line so that it 'flosses' the tunnel from side to side, as you might dry your back with a towel, and work your way from one end to the other and back. Once this is done, repeat the process without the back-and-forth movement; this is because unless your film is absolutely taut the back-and-forth movement tends to miss any natural creases that form under pressure. Depending on the width of the tunnel you may find that your sheet is not long enough to clean the whole upper surface at one go, in which case adjust the line so that you concentrate on one side at a time.

As with washing a car, hose off the dirty water before it has a chance to dry on again. If the day is warm, it may be best to clean the tunnel in sections.

Now that the top of the tunnel is done, use the carwash brush to clean the sides. Wet them first with the hose, then brush them thoroughly but gently, dipping the brush back into the detergent solution at intervals. Finally, hose off the muck.

The inside of the tunnel film should also be washed, as should any staging and so on, and this should be done in the morning to give the film a chance to dry before temperatures fall. As well as increasing light transmission, this reduces the chance of fungal infections present at the end of the last season from overwintering successfully. Note that lacking rainfall, the inside of the tunnel is highly susceptible to toxin build-up – which is why it is so important to use an organic, plant-safe detergent.

Repairing small tears

No matter how careful you are, sooner or later an accident is bound to befall your beloved tunnel. Whether it is a carelessly-wielded length of bamboo or a snag from a passing armful of brambles destined for the compost heap, wear and tear is a part of life – but it's important to be prepared for mishaps by having a roll of polythene repair tape to hand.

A small hole in the cover can quickly spread to form a large tear, particularly if assisted by a high wind. Repairing a large tear rarely gives a long-lasting result, so act as soon as the damage is noticed by applying a patch of repair tape, inside *and* out. If you do have to repair a longer tear, do so by running 'stitches' across the tear to stabilize it, and then run a second piece of tape lengthwise along the tear. Finally, run an extra 'stitch' above and below the tear since these areas will already be under greater stress than the rest of the cover.

Replacing the cover

With some care, polytunnel covers can last a long time; manufacturers typically guarantee them for five years, so one can reasonably expect to get six or seven from them before patching becomes pointless or light transmission has fallen below what you can accept. Re-covering the tunnel is exactly the same as putting on the cover for the first time, so consult the instructions provided by the original manufacturer (or, failing that, read the instructions for covering a DIY tunnel on pp.40-44).

Buying a new cover gives you a slightly wider choice of suppliers than those available for your original purchase because there are a few retailers offering covers only. These can be cheaper than covers purchased from kit manufacturers, but compare specifications carefully to make sure you are not buying an inferior film. Above all, look at the guarantees – if a retailer isn't prepared to say how long they expect a cover to last, assume that it won't last long!

If you can find your original receipt, the size of the supplied cover may well be on it. If not, throw a tape measure over the top of the tunnel and measure the circumference, then add 1.8m (6') to allow for trenching in – or a little less for base rails. This gives the width of film needed, and the length needed is worked out by adding the length and the width of the tunnel together.

You may also need to purchase a new roll of repair tape (it has a finite shelf-life) and some new anti-hotspot tape, as the existing tape will probably be failing. Taking tired tape off the tunnel frame is a tedious job, but some retailers supply anti-hotspot *repair* tape, which saves time because it is applied on top of the original layer.

Chapter 3

Self-build Tunnels

Polytunnel retailers do their best to make things as easy for their customers as possible, and their prices are such that there is seldom any great saving to be made by opting for a Do-It-Yourself (DIY) version. Having said this, sometimes the DIY option is the most suitable; perhaps you have access to materials at a discount; or can obtain suitable waste materials from another project; perhaps you have a modification in mind; or perhaps you're just the practical type who prefers to build things from scratch. The basic structure of a polytunnel is extremely simple, after all; a row of hoops fixed onto stakes, a ridge-pole, a door frame or two, and some means of securing the cover.

The first stage in constructing a DIY tunnel is to work out a materials list, starting with the size of tunnel you would like to build. It's important to think laterally – for instance, one respondent to our polytunnel questionnaire strengthened an inexpensive carport kit and replaced its cover with polythene. It is still doing well three years later.

To help get you started, here is a sample materials list together with instructions for making a simple 3.5m x 6m (12'x 20') tunnel with a door at each end. This is the easiest sort of tunnel to make, since there are no straight-side sections, and a comparatively low ridge height of around 2.1m (7'). The tunnel profile allows it to shed rain and snow well. Since it is held in position with rebar ground stakes and has a distance between hoops of only 1.2m (4'), it is extremely strong.

Materials

- Twelve 90cm (3') lengths of 25mm (1") rebar
- Seven 6m (20') lengths of 50mm (2") PVC pipe
- Five 100mm x 50mm x 2.4m (4"x 2"x 8') lengths pressure-treated timber, planed all round or well sanded
- Five 50mm x 25mm x 2.7m (2" x 1" x 9') lengths pressure-treated timber, planed all round or well sanded

- Three 2m (6' 6") lengths of timber batten
- Duct tape
- Nylon baling twine
- Anti-hotspot tape
- Cover
- A roll of builder's band
- 15cm (6") wood screws
- 50mm (2") wood screws
- Box of tacks

Preparations

Clear the tunnel footprint of vegetation, including the 90cm (3') of clear space around it, and apply the 3,4,5 triangle to mark out the corners of the frame, just as described for commercial installations on pp.25-6. Make sure that you choose a warm day before going any further. This is because you want your PVC piping to be as warm and flexible as possible – so lay it out in the sun.

Construct the frame

The hoops

1. Hammer a length of rebar 45cm (18") into the ground at each corner of one end of the tunnel. You will need to angle them inwards slightly, so that the top leans in towards the ridge line a little (around 15°), which will make it very much easier to slip the PVC pipe over the ends. As you work, use a spirit level to make sure that rebars don't lean towards either end of the tunnel – only towards the ridge line.

2. Once you're happy with the first rebar stakes, gently bend a piece of the PVC pipe into an arch so that you can position the ends directly over the ends of the rebar, and slip the pipe over them. Do not release the tension on the pipe until you have it down to ground level, and make sure that everyone involved in this procedure understands that it could be dangerous to let go before the pipe is in position.

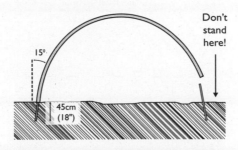

Don't
stand
here!

15°

45cm
(18")

DIY – the hoops

3. Once the first hoop is in position, you should have some idea of what angle of rebar suits your installation, so hammer in the rebar stakes at the other end of the tunnel.

4. Use a string line and measuring tape to mark every 1.2m (4') along the sides of the tunnel.

5. Hammer in the remaining pieces of rebar as before, and then push a piece of PVC pipe onto each pair of stakes. You will now begin to see how much space your tunnel will give you – if you're going to change your mind about the length, now's the time.

The ridge-pole

1. Use a tape measure to find the exact middle of the tunnel at each end, and run a tight string between these two points to mark the tunnel's midline.

2. Using a plumb line (any weight on the end of a piece of string), find and mark the point on each hoop that is directly above the midline.

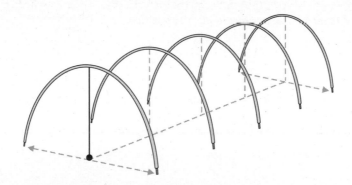

Use a plumb line to find the mid-point on each hoop

3. Position the last section of pipe along the underside of the hoops so that it runs along the marked midpoints, and secure it temporarily with tape or string so that it does not sag.

4. This pipe will act as the tunnel's ridge-pole, so, using a narrow drill bit, make a pilot hole up through it at each of the points where it meets a hoop; make sure that the ridge-pole does not stick out further than the hoops at each end, or it will rub through the film in no time. The pilot-hole should go right through the ridge-pole and one wall of the hoops only, but it's not the end of the world if you go right through by accident.

5. Drive a 50mm (2") screw up through each of the pilot holes, leaving the head just exposed.

6. Use a length of baling twine to lash each of the intersections. This is done by putting a slipknot (or similar) near one end of the length, passing it over the head of the screw and pulling tight, and then wrapping the baling twine around the joint in an X-shape. Half a dozen wraps in each direction should be plenty, but remember that effective lashing has to be kept very tight until you secure the loose end by tying it off on the screw head, or by knotting it with the other end of the twine.

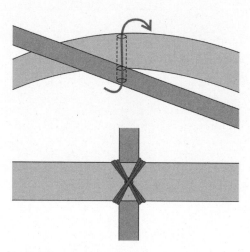

Securing the intersections of ridge-pole and hoops

NOTE: If you find you dislike lashing, two zip-ties in an X-shape around the intersection will work just as well, although you will need to put duct tape over the top to cushion the film.

Doors

Construct the doors

1. To make each door, cut two pieces of 25mm x 50mm (1" x 2") timber to provide two 1.8m (6') lengths for the sides, and three 85cm (2' 9") lengths to act as top, bottom and mid-rail. Assemble the pieces on a flat surface with the timbers sitting edge-on rather than flat (see diagram below). The top and bottom of the door should be flush with and between the uprights, and the mid-rail around 70cm (2' 4") from the top of the door.

2. Using a narrow drill bit, mark and drill the pilot holes through the door sides and into the cross-pieces. You will need to allow TWO holes for the end of each cross-piece, so that they cannot rotate. Once this is done, use a wider drill bit to widen the first 3mm (⅛") of each hole so that the screws will be countersunk.

3. Screw the door together, making sure that none of the screw heads protrude.

4. Repeat for the door at the other end of the tunnel.

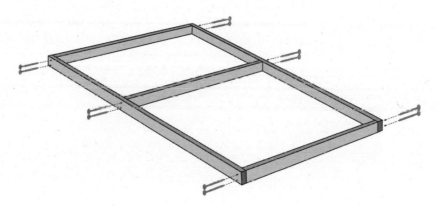

Constructing the door

Construct the door frames

1. To make each door frame, lay one of the 2.4m (8') timbers down on each side of a prepared door on a flat surface. These will be the frame uprights.

2. Measure so that the top edge of the door is 30cm (1') away from the top end of the uprights.

3. One of the timbers should be touching the door, but on the other side use the barrel of a hinge as a spacer at each end of the door, and press the timber uprights against these spacers. This is to create enough clearance for the door to open and close against the frame.

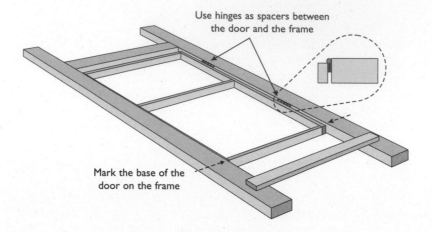

Use hinges as spacers between the door and the frame

Mark the base of the door on the frame

4. Mark and cut another of the 2.4m (8') timbers to just fit between the frame uprights and position it snugly against the top of the door to form a lintel. Check that it is the same distance from the end of each of the frame uprights, and put two screws through the uprights into the lintel using pilot holes, as you did during the making of the doors.

5. Making sure that the uprights are still snug against the door and spacers, cut and nail a piece of batten between them, a few inches from the bottom end. Don't worry about how this looks, since it will be buried along with the bottom of the uprights.

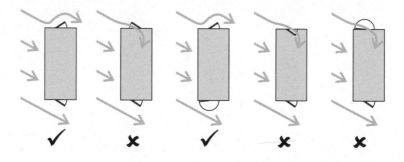

Door orientation and wind direction

6. Decide which upright the door will be hinged to, and whether the door will open inwards or outwards; primarily this is decided by the direction in which any strong winds are likely to strike your tunnel, but bear in mind that inward opening doors require a clear space to open into.

7. Attach the door to the frame using the hinges, and allowing at least 4mm clearance at the top.

8. Once you have the door working correctly, mark both the door and the frame to indicate which end of the tunnel they are for. Also mark the position of the bottom of the door clearly on the frame uprights, as you will need to be able to see this when you erect the frame. Once this is done, take the door off and store safely, and repeat the door frame construction for the other end of the tunnel.

9. Finally, cut two 75cm (30") pieces of batten, which you will need to secure the cover to the frame tops later.

Erect the door frames

1. Dig a trench along each end of the tunnel, in line with the rebar stakes supporting the end hoop. The trench should be centred on the midline of the tunnel and be both long and deep enough to take the frame, so that the level of the bottom of the door (marked clearly on the frame uprights) is clear of the ground. Do not worry about the uprights being too high, as these will be trimmed to size at the top later.

2. Stand the frame in the hole at intervals until it is deep enough, then centre it on the midline.

3. Use a spirit level to make sure that the frame is level in both directions, and then mark the uprights under the end hoop and cut them to this mark.

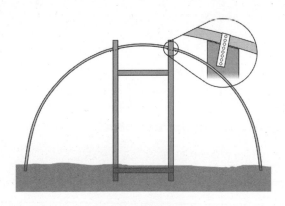

Erecting the door

4. Sand the cut ends well, and then put the frame back into position. Fix it to the end hoop at each corner by bending a length of builders' band over the hoop and tacking it onto the wood on both sides.

5. Recheck the levels of the frame before backfilling the trench, taking care to tamp the earth down properly around the uprights.

Trenching

Dig a 30cm x 30cm (1' x 1') trench all around the tunnel with the exception of the doorways. The trench should run 15cm (6") outside the tunnel perimeter for the sides, and turn round the ends where it tapers in towards the door frames, as shown below. Trenching in the edges of the cover is the strongest way to secure the whole structure, with the weight of backfill making it almost impossible for the wind to lift.

Shape of trench around the polytunnel

Covering the tunnel

Always pick a still, warm, dry day to cover your tunnel. If there is more than the lightest of breezes the cover will be less manageable, and your end result will be looser and more prone to damage. Also, make sure you have plenty of help; although it is theoretically possible to put a cover on with just two people, some stages will be awkward. Four people is ideal, but make sure that they can stay for as long as you need them. Getting tension around the doorways is the trickiest part, so don't end up doing it on your own.

1. While your helpers get themselves organised, take a look at the tunnel frame that you have made. Use a step-ladder to get a good look at the top surface. The film will pass over the outside of the structure, so there should be no rough edges or scuffs to chafe it; if you find any, now is the time to run a layer or two of duct tape over them until you are happy that they will not scratch the film. This may be necessary at either end of the ridge-pole, depending on how neatly you screwed it on, and you will certainly have to tape over the builder's band well.

2. Covers with film coating on them must be fitted the right way up and have printing on them to help you determine this, so check the cover manufacturer's instructions before you go any further. Unpack your cover on the windward side of the tunnel and put the receipt away safely. If there are any sticks or stones that might damage it, cover them with sheeting before you take the cover out of its box.

3. Arrange the cover so that it will unfold or unroll easily as you pull it, and then muster all your helpers to slide it smoothly over the frame. This is the most dangerous point for the cover so make sure everyone has a good grip; if a gust of wind catches you unawares, you could find yourself briefly flying the most expensive kite you have ever owned.

4. Working quickly, centre the film over the frame so that there is an even amount of surplus at each side, and at each end. Make sure all the folds are open, but don't worry too much about tension for now. You'll notice you only have enough spare film at the ends to reach halfway to the ground, but don't panic; the fill for the end panels comes mainly from the sides, not the top.

5. To keep the film still for the moment, push it into the corners of the trench and weight it down with some backfill, and then do the same in the middle of each side. By the time you have done this at least one of your helpers will have ventured inside the tunnel, so take a moment to join them – you'll find that the temperature inside has already started to climb, and from here on it's just a matter of making things secure and neat. Now is an excellent time to have a cup of tea – not least because the greenhouse effect will warm up the cover for you, making it easier to tension.

Securing and tightening

The less play that there is on a polytunnel cover, the longer it will last. Cover film is strong and does stretch to a certain extent, but try to avoid grabbing and yanking because this is apt to cause grip marks. For this reason, when stretching the film always make sure that you only hold sections that are going to be buried or trimmed off later.

1. Check that the film is properly centred on the frame.

2. Take one of the 75cm (30") lengths of batten and put two tacks partway through it in the middle, about 15cm (6") apart. Smooth the cover over one of the end hoops and use the batten to trap it against the outside of the frame.

3. Hammer the two tacks home so that the film is held firm, without any pleats or creases between the tacks.

4. Repeat this process at the other end of the tunnel, but this time have one of your helpers take hold of the end of the film and actually stretch it along the length, leaving you to smooth it out before using the batten and two tacks to trap it against the top of the frame, as before. Do not tack the rest of the batten down just yet.

5. Backfill the trench, starting at the middle of the most visible side of your tunnel (as this first side is likely to look neater). Have your helpers position the film so that it runs into the trench and back out again, creating a gutter into which the backfill goes. At this stage you are only aiming to put a little tension on the film, and to ease it over the hoops to minimize creasing. Work out from the middle to one end, half-filling the trench as you go.

6. Where the trench turns inward towards the door frame, you will need to cut a slit in the cover to enable you to turn the corner neatly. This should run from the outside edge of the cover in towards the corner, stopping an inch or so underground for neatness. Stop backfilling once the corner is done.

7. Repeat this process for the second side, but this time you need to put more tension on the film. Rather than letting it go right down to the bottom of the trench, have your helpers hold the gutter of film up a little as you shovel the backfill in, so that the weight of the soil – helped by your foot – stretches the film downwards as you work. Once again only half-fill the trench and make sure you ease the film over the hoops, smoothing it out from the centre and downwards as you work.

A pleated corner

8. Now that both sides are held firmly, secure the film around the remainder of the door frame. Because you are gathering the film in to a relatively narrow doorway it has to be pleated as shown on the diagram on the previous page. Bend the top batten away from the door frame gently and start to pleat, working outwards from the middle, with a helper keeping the spare film under gentle tension as you work. Note that pleating creates pockets in which water will collect, so you should pleat so that these are on the outside of the tunnel. Collecting rainwater outside is less of a problem than collecting an unpleasant soup of condensation, dead insects and mould inside.

NOTE: The pleats should be concentrated around the corners of the frame (see diagram opposite) for the neatest and tightest cover, and don't be afraid to have several goes at this.

9. Once you reach the end of the batten and are happy with it, have your helpers increase the tension, and fix the batten to the frame by hammering in a tack every 10cm (4"). Do not put a tack in the last 7.5cm (3") in case the batten splits; if you think it needs a final tack, then pre-drill a hole through it with a narrow drill bit.

10. Repeat for the other side of the top of the frame, checking that you have the pleating more or less symmetrical before tacking it down.

11. Use another suitable length of batten to trap the film against each doorpost. Pleat as before, remembering that the pockets should be on the outside. Your helpers should provide as much tension as possible until the tacking is finished.

12. Once both doorposts have been tacked, finish tensioning and half-backfilling the trench at the end of the polytunnel, and repeat for the other end. If any section of the cover seems in need of more tension, then pull it outwards at that point and tread the cover back down into the trench.

13. Once you are happy with it, trim the film to just below ground level all the way round the outside edge of the trench, and remove any excess inside the doorways.

NOTE: Spare polytunnel film is recyclable through your local authority, or anywhere that accepts plastic bags. However, sizeable pieces are very useful in the garden for a variety of purposes including the making of home-made cloches, so think twice before you dispose of it.

14. To prevent water run-off from the tunnel collecting in the buried film gutter, drive a garden fork through the cover at the bottom of the trench at intervals. Once this is done complete the backfilling all the way round and tread the earth down as hard as you can.

Fitting the doors

15. Cut some of the excess cover film to provide squares a little larger than the panels of the doors, and secure them to the outside of the door with tacks.

16. Once this is done, cut sections of batten to size and nail the battens down hard onto the frames, so that the film is trapped between the batten and the frame.

NOTE: Some tunnel owners prefer to use some netting for the upper section of their doors, to improve ventilation. If you do this it is still a good idea to allow for a removable piece of cover film to go over the netting in winter; this can be a slightly oversized roll-up section secured at the top with a piece of batten, or a neat picture-frame affair that can come off entirely for the summer.

17. Fit each door onto the correct end of the tunnel, adjusting ground level as necessary.

18. Fix a catch onto the outside of the door you will normally use to enter your tunnel, and another onto the inside of the other door – so that you cannot accidentally trap yourself inside.

19. Depending on how windy your site gets, you might choose to fit some extra door furniture. A drop bolt is extremely secure, but even in very sheltered sites you should hammer in timber stakes to limit how far the doors can move, to prevent accidental damage to the cover and frames.

Using recycled materials

Because they do not use plastic film, shade tunnels are very easy to self-build. Pat Bowcock, the owner of the organic vegetable business 'Ourganics' in Dorset, UK, is a keen permaculturist and well used to making things on the fly. When a friend gave her a sizeable piece of shade mesh that was surplus to requirements, she saw the potential to build a shade house – the perfect environment for seedlings and young plants.

So, on a showery day in late April, we packed our waterproofs and turned out to lend a hand.

Pat's preference was to use recycled materials whenever possible, and in her 'useful materials' corner we uncovered a roll of 20mm (0.8") flexible plastic water pipe. This is not rigid enough to use for one-piece hoops, but we also found an assortment of metal pipes culled from a recycling centre. We decided to use these to make straight sides for the shade tunnel, and to use the plastic piping with some additional vertical supports for the hooped upper section. To do this, we cut the available tubes into lengths of around 1.5m (5'), and identified the strongest pieces to form the ends of the tunnel. Using the 3,4,5 triangle (see pp.25-26) we marked out the structure's footprint and pushed the corner tubes 30cm (1') into the ground at an angle (leaning in at roughly 15°), and then marked and positioned tubes for all the intermediate hoops. Although Pat's shade tunnel was situated in a sheltered spot and she intended to remove the netting during the winter, the site is occasionally subject to severe gales. With that in mind, we positioned the hoops only 90cm (3') apart, and left four sections of tube to act as diagonal braces for the end hoops.

After experimenting with different lengths of the 20mm pipe we settled on one which gave a head height of around 2m (6' 6") allowing for a 15cm (6") overlap on each tube, and set them in position before drilling and screwing into pilot holes made with a suitable metal bit. This gave us the tunnel shape. We marked the tunnel's midline on the ground and used a plumb line hanging from each hoop to find and mark the middle of each hoop section. This gave the position of the ridge-pole, for which we selected a length of light but strong nylon fibre pole found in an industrial scrap store, similar to the struts in a modern tent. We drilled pilot holes at measured intervals along the ridge-pole and at the marked centre positions on each hoop, supported the ridge-pole temporarily with tape, and then securely wired it into place.

Bracing and guy ropes

Once this was done, we fitted diagonal bracing by bolting a section of tube from halfway up each end hoop to the base of an intermediate hoop on the same side, which stops the end hoops from flexing in and out. For added lateral strength we ran guy ropes of polypropylene twine from the high end of each diagonal brace diagonally outward, so that the structure was stretched outwards in all directions.

After looking at the shade netting, Pat asked us to use a double thickness of it. Since this would weigh quite a bit when wet, we added vertical supports in the form of aluminium tubes (part of the frame of a long-dead gazebo) topped with Y-shaped pieces of locally-cut hazel, in which the ridge-pole rested. We draped the double thickness of shade netting over the frame, weighted it at the edges with suitable timber and secured it to the end hoops with twists of wire. We left it open at the north end for ease of access, and allowed an extra length at the south end. This extra length can be pegged at ground level to create a closed end, pulled outwards onto uprights to form a canopy, or rolled up when it is not needed.

We visited Pat again in a spell of hot, sunny weather later that year and found the shade tunnel full of staging, with trays of salad and tiny herb seedlings. Pat told us that the tunnel had shrugged off some recent gales with no damage. "It's revolutionised my mornings," she told us. "Until the tunnel went up, modules for hardening off had to be moved under cover during the hottest part of the day to prevent scorch – no joke when you have five dozen trays to move."

Chapter 4

The Tunnel Environment

From the first moment that you step into your polytunnel, even before you have finished fixing the cover around the door frames, you will realise that you are in a different climate from the world outside. Sheltered, warm and humid, the interior of a polytunnel can feel like summer even in early spring thanks to the greenhouse effect. Yet for as long as the cover is in position no rain will fall on the soil, and the environmental changes may benefit some pests and diseases – so it is important to understand about the new climate zone that you are creating within your garden.

Soil as a living thing

In these days of chemical gardening and hydroponic crop production, there is a tendency to think of soil as an inert substance into which we plant crops. Indeed, some high-value crops such as giant hybrid strawberries are so susceptible to moulds and soil-borne diseases that the farmers need to sterilize the soil with toxic fumigants in order to produce a viable crop. But there are problems with this approach. Plants growing on sterile soil are less able to shrug off infestations and infections, and thus need frequent applications of pesticides and fungicides. Furthermore, after the first one or two growing seasons the soil becomes depleted of nutrients, and without vigorous application of nutrient supplements it becomes worthless dirt.

To novices, gardening seems to be all about plants: choosing varieties, getting sowing and planting times right, and watering to perfection. While all these things are important, any experienced gardener will tell you that it is all about *soil*. Soil is a bustling, thriving ecosystem, more complicated and robust than any rainforest. However, most of the life in your garden is out of sight beneath the soil surface. From earthworms and millipedes down to actinomycetes and fungi, each has its role to play in the constant building and renewal of a vital resource for your plants: healthy soil.

In a forest environment, there are a number of inputs that the soil needs in order to stay healthy: rainfall, leaf-fall, and additional minerals from rock erosion and other sources. Within the sheltered confines of the tunnel *you* must provide these inputs, avoid the application of toxins, and monitor the soil itself from time to time to make sure that you are getting things right. These are all tasks that gardeners are well used to performing, but in a tunnel the consequences of casual neglect are far more serious.

Bedding options

When deciding what type of bed to use for growing your plants there are several options, each with its own advantages and disadvantages. With the exception of container growing, it is much easier to dig out and pre-pare these beds shortly before the cover goes on to your tunnel, since manoeuvring a wheelbarrow will be simpler and you do not have to worry about accidentally piercing the film.

Soil beds

The simplest option, traditional *soil beds* are preferably prepared by double-digging and the incorporation of organic matter. Double-digging involves taking the topsoil off a strip of ground to the depth of a spade blade to form a trench, and putting it to one side so that the soil under-neath it can be dug over with a garden fork. Organic material is lightly forked into the bottom of the trench. The top spade's depth of a neigh-bouring strip is used to backfill the first trench and the process continued, until finally the set-aside from the first trench is used to backfill the last trench. However, if you discover that you do not have a sufficient depth of topsoil then you must either dig out the subsoil and replace it with imported topsoil, or consider creating a *raised bed* (see diagram p.50).

Raised beds

A raised bed involves piling soil or a soil/compost mix higher than the level of the surrounding ground. This is usually done in a wide strip of up to 1.2m (4') – any wider and reaching the middle without treading on the soil (discouraged because of damage to the soil structure) becomes difficult. If you are raising the soil level by 15cm (6") or less then there is no need to construct a frame to contain the soil, which can simply be mounded up with gently-sloping sides to make a *soft-edged bed*. Beyond this height the shape becomes impossible to maintain and a frame of brickwork, blocks or boards is needed to contain the soil, making a *hard-edged bed*. If your tunnel is set on a concrete surface, then a 45cm (18") raised bed is quite possible.

Hard-edged raised beds are useful because they put less strain on the lower back than working at ground level. Compost and other remedial applications stay confined within the frame, keeping paths cleaner.

However, raised beds drain faster than soil beds so it is doubly important to keep the soil rich in moisture-retaining organic material. Furthermore, the gaps in and around the framework of a hard-edged bed provide easy sheltering points for slugs, which are likely to be more of a problem in this situation. It is worth pointing out that soft-edged beds are less work in a polytunnel than they are outside, where heavy rainfall is constantly eroding the edges.

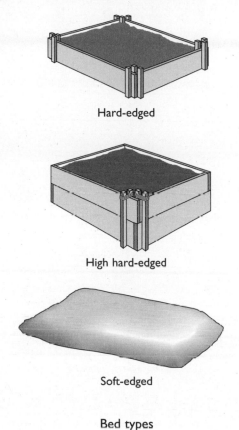

Hard-edged

High hard-edged

Soft-edged

Bed types

Making raised beds is easier than double-digging. Firstly plan the beds, remembering that anything wider than 1.2m (4') will require a stretch or a stepping-stone to reach the middle. If you will be working between two raised beds, a path of 60cm (2') will be needed to kneel down comfortably, and considerably more if you plan on bringing manure in with a wheelbarrow in the future. Also, the overhang of plants onto the path may make this a damp journey in times of heavy dew, at which time you also risk spreading disease and/or pests from plant to plant. Measure the distances between the corners, and cut boards or planks to run between them. You will also need a number of sharpened stakes to support these boards at intervals of 1m (3′). The frames will eventually rot, although it is possible to treat the wood with a suitable plant-safe preservative such as Osmo Wood Protector.

Mark the corners of the bed and dig it over to loosen the soil to the depth of the spade's blade, being careful to remove the roots of any perennial weeds. Fork in a generous amount of compost or manure (*figure 1, below*). Lay the boards on the soil to establish the edges, and hammer the supporting stakes in (*figure 2*). Lean the boards upright against the stakes, then fill the bed with a mixture of topsoil and organic matter (*figure 3*). There is no need to fix the boards to the stakes as the weight of the soil will do this for you, but if you are making the bed more than one board high, or if your soil is very heavy, then using a second set of stakes inside the bed is helpful, since the boards are held between the inner and outer stakes. The pairs of stakes may be tied or wired together at the top.

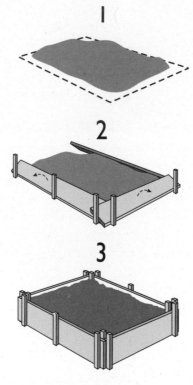

Making a raised bed

Container growing

This is a very popular choice for greenhouses and polytunnels alike. Most plants can be container-grown through the whole of their lives, starting in tiny modules and ending in massive pots or grow-bags; however, a multitude of pots and the inevitable compost bags create a multitude of hiding-places – not only for slugs and snails, but also for mice and nibbling insects. Unless you are very careful, plants in a tunnel with many containers will suffer considerable damage from such pests. Containers are also troublesome to water unless you invest in micro-irrigation (see p.55) and may have to be watered more than once a day in hot weather. However, if a plant in a container becomes diseased or is attacked by a pest, it can be easily moved into a quarantine/treatment area before the trouble has much of a chance to spread.

Maintaining soil health

Over the growing season, the complex ecosystem of your soil gradually uses up the organic matter within it, and the soil level will actually slump a little each year as crops grow. This is an entirely natural process and not something to be opposed. In an unmanaged ecosystem this would be offset by the accumulation of leaf-fall and other debris, with grazing animals contributing to the available minerals with their dung. There are no substantial ecosystems on earth that do not rely on animals for this contribution, and it is probably no coincidence that animals evolved before land plants.

Beds under cultivation are largely cut off from these inputs, and it is up to you to supply them. The use of organic matter is particularly important since it is this, in the form of stable humus, which acts as a sponge to help the soil to retain its moisture. Whether or not you practise a formal crop rotation in your tunnel, this means that each bed will need an application of 7.5-10cm (3"-4") of well-rotted manure every three or four years, and a similar depth of seed-free compost in all the other years. This should be done as soon as summer plantings are taken out in the autumn or early winter, and they can be lightly forked into the surface layer if you need the area for winter planting; otherwise they can simply be laid on top of the beds, remembering that any drip hose will need to be raised gently to be just below the new surface. Provided that watering is kept up over the winter, the earthworms and other life in the soil will gradually incorporate this top-dressing for you, and by the spring there will be no sign of it apart from a fibrous and open texture to the soil surface – ideal for planting.

Usually these additions are all that the soil requires, and even hungry plants like tomatoes should need little extra feeding. However, it takes time to bring soil up to this level of health, and for this reason for the first few years you should supply a dusting of a natural mineral supplement such as volcanic rock dust at the same time as the compost and manure.

Furthermore, to begin with you should watch your plants for any signs that your soil is low in certain minerals such as magnesium (lower leaves are yellow with green veins), and be ready to take remedial action.

For further reading on the organic management of a healthy soil, we recommend *Organic Gardening: The Natural No-dig Way* by Charles Dowding (see *Appendix 2: Further Reading*).

Water in the tunnel

We have already touched on the importance of watering from day one. This is because although the tunnel cover provides absolute shelter from rain, it does not stop evaporation of water from the soil surface, nor the drying out of the soil by thirsty plants, known as transpiration. On a hot summer day, a mature tomato plant can easily pull two litres of water out of the soil around it. Obviously this means that the watering requirements for a bed or container vary with the type and number of plants in it, and this means that the different beds in your tunnel will need different amounts of water.

In strong sunlight, the inside of a polytunnel can get very hot indeed. Plants are able to withstand these high temperatures well, but only if they are kept well watered – forget to do it at your peril. The amounts of water needed in hot weather are quite considerable, and for this reason it is **vital** to have a source of water no more than a few steps away from the tunnel. This is so important that it is best to consider where the water is going to come from at the planning stage (see *Planning Your Purchase*, p.12).

Mains water

This is obviously very convenient if you can provide it. Usually chlorinated to kill fungi and bacteria, it is always there (literally 'on tap') and needs no treatment before being applied to plants. However, rising energy costs mean that tap water is likely to become a more expensive resource as time passes, and water companies are increasingly keen to meter household usage. It therefore makes sense to conserve this precious resource, and at the very least prepare for any shortfall in supply.

Rainwater

This can be collected from the roof of any nearby structure and stored in barrels, butts or tanks, which should all be covered to help prevent the supply from being colonized by algae and other organisms and to stop visiting creatures from falling in. You should do what you can to stop leaves, twigs and other debris from ending up in the butts; there are commercial systems available, but even an old sock tied over the end of the downspout will do a fairly good job provided it is cleaned regularly. If the storage vessels are kept covered the water inside should remain in good condition, but they will need to be cleaned out once every year or two. Should the water inside them begin to smell swampy, it is a good idea to disinfect or 'sweeten' the water by adding a measured dose of a suitable natural, non-biocidal product such as Citrox or a few crystals of potassium permanganate.

Greywater

Greywater is water that has already been used for washing. This includes water from laundry, baths, showers, hand washing etc., but not toilet waste (commonly called black water). Greywater is not suitable for use in the polytunnel, because the increased levels of nitrogen and phosphates in the water can quickly build up to toxic levels in the soil. However, it makes very little sense to discard all of the treated water that we use simply because it has a little soap and dirt in it, and greywater can be used safely for irrigation provided certain rules are followed. Although outside the scope of this book, learning to use greywater in the garden will improve your water security and reduce the use of your precious rainwater, and so we heartily recommend it (see *Appendix 2: Further Reading*, p.116). *If you have not learned about greywater systems, do not use greywater to irrigate food crops.*

Irrigation

The best time to apply water, as with elsewhere in the garden, is in the evening. Plants with deep roots are able to pull water up from deeper layers of the soil, but for smaller plants or those with shallow root systems (such as lettuce) watering in the evening allows more time for the plant to draw up water than a morning application. However, evening watering also creates perfect conditions for slugs to move about, and if they are a problem in your tunnel, it may be necessary to water early in the morning instead. There are many ways in which the water can be applied. It is of course possible to get by using only a watering-can, but in high summer using a can alone is quite labour-intensive, except in very small tunnels. This is why most tunnel gardeners choose a combination of watering methods to help them fine-tune the moisture for each individual plant.

Overhead sprinklers

These are a common sight in commercial tunnels, and it is for this reason that many tunnel manufacturers include them in their catalogues. They are simple to install provided you have mains access, but there are drawbacks to their use. The most important of these is that the water is applied indiscriminately to all plants. This is not a problem in a commercial application simply because the grower is generally raising large numbers of the same variety, but in a smaller situation like a community farm or a home tunnel there may be thirsty tomatoes on one side of a path and a hardy lemon tree on the other – two plants with very different requirements.

A second problem is that water drips from the sprinklers at the end of the watering cycle, potentially causing soil splash (a trigger for fungal infection) to plants underneath them. This can be prevented simply by attaching a length of string to the bottom of the sprinkler head, so that the water runs down the string to the earth without a splash. The water from a sprinkler system also tends to be concentrated in a pattern around the sprinkler heads themselves. Although this can be minimized by careful adjustment of the water pressure, it is still necessary to finish the job off by hand with a hose or watering-can. Finally, using an overhead sprinkler system to soak the whole tunnel raises the humidity, for which reason it has to be done in the early part of the day, giving plants without deep roots less time to take up the water before things start to dry out again.

Overhead misters

These are set up in a similar way to sprinkler systems and the same caveats apply, but misters use some added electronics to produce a fine fog of tiny droplets which evaporate quickly in the heat of the day. In this case the aim is to cool the tunnel and raise humidity, often as a control measure for red spider mites, rather than to irrigate.

Drip hoses (also known as 'seep-' or 'soaker-hoses')

Drip hoses are a common solution to the time-consuming nature of watering in a polytunnel. Like overhead sprinklers they are indiscriminate in the amount of water that they supply, but if they are laid just below the surface of the soil or under a generous layer of mulch the water takes longer to evaporate. In addition, they have a much less humidifying effect on the air in the tunnel and so can be used at night with a clockwork or electronic timer. A drip hose is more effective and lasts longer if it is laid just beneath the surface of the soil by making a trench for it with a trowel.

At its simplest, a drip hose is simply a length of pipe with tiny holes driven through it, but such systems tend to deliver more water at the point where they are connected to the supply, leaving the other end comparatively dry. More sophisticated systems that overcome this problem involve hose made from porous recycled rubber, or hosepipe with internal drippers. These solutions all have different water pressure require-ments, so choose carefully; some work best from the mains supply, with or without a pressure regulator, whereas some can be run successfully from a water barrel. With the latter, the amount of header space (the vertical distance between the bottom of the supply container and the highest point of the hose) varies considerably.

Micro-irrigation

This is available from specialist irrigation suppliers, and can supplement other watering solutions with adjustable drippers and misters supplying the needs of individual plants. This is a relatively expensive option, but allows for very fine control of automated watering, even while you are away on holiday. Given the breadth of equipment available for profes-sional growers, it is possible to be as technical as you like in your irrigation, with humidity sensors and multiple-zone timers – at a price.

Capillary beds

A capillary bed is a handy way of keeping an entire bench full of plants moist for several days without attention. This uses the tendency of water to creep along any porous material to provide a constantly moist surface on which you can stand pots and trays, and provided plants are correctly potted and well-watered before putting them on the bed, there should be no need for any further watering. This can be a blessing, particularly when bringing on seedlings that cannot tolerate drying out, but top-watering once a week is advisable to stop nutrients from becoming con-centrated at the surface of the compost. Because they keep containers so wet, capillary beds are not suitable for winter use or for plants that need to dry out a little between waterings, such as fuchsias and succulents.

To make a capillary bed, begin by setting up a reservoir of water such as an inverted plastic container sitting in a large plant saucer. You will need to drill a hole through the container about 1cm (or half an inch) away from the rim. Fill the container with fresh water, place the plant saucer upside-down over the top and, holding both of them carefully, invert the whole thing. Water will pour out of the container through the drilled hole until the water level just covers it. This reservoir will need to be positioned so that the plant saucer is below the capillary matting by 2.5-10cm (1"-4") so that the matting can pull the water from the reservoir, but not flood the bench. One way of achieving this is to use a thick sheet of expanded polystyrene to give the height that you need, but if you have two sections of staging then one can be raised on lengths of 5cm (2") timber, and the reservoir placed on the other.

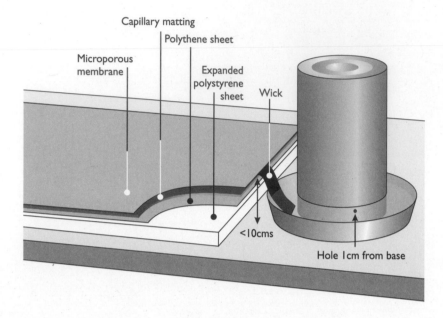

Capillary matting

Polythene sheet

Microporous membrane

Expanded polystyrene sheet

Wick

<10cms

Hole 1cm from base

Capillary bed

Ensure that your staging is fairly level and protect it from moisture with an off-cut of polytunnel cover, or with a section of expanded polystyrene sheeting. Lay a piece of capillary matting on the plastic, having first cut off a piece to use as a wick, and cover it with microporous membrane. This membrane is essential to prevent plants from rooting into the matting, and is often sold with it. Set up the water reservoir near the edge of the matting. Finally tuck one end of the wick under the capillary matting and the other end into the plant saucer – without allowing it to dip in the middle – and give the whole of the capillary matting a good soak with a watering-can.

A watering-can

A watering-can with a fine rose is invaluable in the tunnel. No matter which solution you choose for your irrigation, there, will always be areas of soil, or particular plants, which require that little bit of extra water. Of course a garden hose with a spray attachment can do the same job, but this may be too rough for delicate seedlings and is too indiscriminate for spot-watering on the bench. A wand watering head is also good for localised irrigation, provided it is capable of delivering a gentle shower rather than a jet of water. A watering-can is also handy when applying liquid feed, particularly if you choose one that has a volume indicator on the side.

Conserving water

Polytunnels use a lot of water in hot weather, but this can be reduced by the use of mulch on the soil surface. Mulch creates a humid micro-climate at the soil surface, reducing evaporation and the growth of weeds; suitable materials include straw, bark and shredded unbleached paper, although a 'living mulch' of your favourite ground-cover plant is also an option. Simply apply a 7.5-10cm (3"-4") layer of material over the surface of the beds after a good watering, leaving gaps around the stems of plants. Mulch holds water in the soil, but it also acts as a partial barrier to irrigation from above reaching it (drip hoses laid underneath the mulch do not share this problem). To get around this, top-up watering-can be very gently applied near the stem of plants, in the gap in the mulch. This should be done very gently, using a watering-can with a fine rose. As an alternative for faster watering, a homemade funnel such as an empty, tall plant pot can be bedded into the mulch near thirsty plants like tomatoes, and water poured into that.

There are drawbacks to the use of mulch in tunnels. Slugs are likely to be more of a problem, since it provides a million handy hiding-places and ideal conditions for egg-laying; fungi and moulds also frequently move into the mulch and this can have implications for plant health, although this is less likely to occur in hot summers. Both of these problems can be largely eliminated if a purpose-made mulching fabric is used, provided that it is only weighted with stones so that it can be lifted easily to check for slugs. Biodegradable mulching fabric such as WeedBlock can be applied annually, but is fiddly to use in the gaps between plants.

In outdoor growing, close planting is often recommended to reduce surface evaporation, since an almost continuous canopy of plants reduces the amount of ventilation at the soil surface. In the warmer and more humid environment of a polytunnel, however, this cannot be recommended since these are the precise conditions that favour mould and fungal infections. Instead, try to group thirstier plants such as tomatoes together, so that heavier watering is restricted to specific areas.

Try to resist the urge to water simply because the surface of the soil is dry. On sunny days the surface of polytunnel beds loses moisture very quickly, but this is only a problem for germinating seeds, seedlings, and very shallow-rooted plants; take a trowel and cut straight down in an empty section of bed, and you will often find that the drier topsoil only extends down 25mm (1") or even less. Under these conditions most plants are perfectly able to pull moisture out of the deeper layers of the soil, and even if they look a little tired in the heat of the afternoon, they will soon perk up in the evening. This is particularly a factor when using a drip hose which is laid just beneath the surface of the soil; even when the irrigation has done its work the soil surface looks extremely dry except for a tell-tale trail of moisture over the hose itself, but only spot-watering for the thirstier plants and seedlings is now required.

Watering with the changing seasons

Water requirements in the tunnel vary from day to day depending on the temperature, amount of sunlight, relative humidity, the activity of plants and the amount of ventilation that you provide. In summer, moisture levels in the tunnel must be checked every evening without fail, and damping-down may be necessary during the day if there are any signs of red spider mite (see *Preventing Pests* p.96), whereas you may only need to water lightly and less frequently during the winter. Getting the irrigation of your tunnel right as outside conditions change is therefore something of an art, but one that is easy to master provided you are aware that it needs to be monitored every few days. Using a timer to set up automatic irrigation is a worthwhile investment, but don't assume that once things are going well you can forget about it. A few unusual days in a row and you may find that your beds are waterlogged – or worse, dry as a bone.

For beginners, a simple moisture meter is a good investment. Every few days, dig a small hole at least 10cm (4") deep with a trowel so that you can look at the soil, and touch it with your fingertips before using the moisture meter; learn the appearance and behaviour of properly moist soil. After a while you will learn when it is necessary to shut off the auto-matic supply for a day, or to give things a little extra. You will also work out which areas of the tunnel need regular attention with a watering-can, and little by little you will use the moisture meter less and less. Of course, you can install complete electronic irrigation control systems which use multiple moisture meters to determine exactly how much water the soil needs – but if you have not learned to monitor soil conditions yourself, any breakdowns are likely to be very painful lessons.

Ventilation

In most tunnels, ventilation is provided by simply opening the doors. For small tunnels a single door at one end is sufficient, but for all other models, doors at each end are a definite advantage. This is because adequate ventilation is crucial to control temperature and humidity, two factors that can be problematic in various ways depending on conditions.

As a general rule, one end of the tunnel should be opened each and every morning, and kept open until about an hour before sunset. In terms of temperature, the aim of this is to minimize the difference between daytime and night, since wildly fluctuating temperatures can cause problems with some crops (e.g. tomatoes). Allowing an hour of closed temperature build-up in the evening means that the tunnel takes longer to cool down; but after dawn, relative humidity in the tunnel is high and temperatures may rise faster outside it than inside. This is especially evident in winter, when the early-morning tunnel seems like another, rather misty, little world.

In hot or humid conditions, open both ends of larger tunnels to allow some airflow straight through, except on windy days. Lowering the relative humidity in the tunnel reduces the growth of moulds and fungi, and allows plants to cool themselves by evaporating water from their leaves more efficiently.

The only time that tunnel doors should remain shut all day is in winter when the outside temperature is not expected to rise above freezing. Under these conditions open the doors briefly in the early morning to expel the very cold air trapped in the tunnel, and then close them to let the greenhouse effect do its work.

Heat

There is no doubt that providing artificial heat in your tunnel, particularly in early spring, allows for earlier production of tender crops, and yet in terms of energy efficiency and carbon emissions it is far better to transport food from a few hundred miles south than it is to heat an entire tunnel. This is not to say that there is nothing that you can do to boost temperatures – far from it.

As with any dwelling, stopping draughts is very important to prevent any heat accumulated in the daytime from simply dribbling away as the outside temperature drops. Unless your tunnel is fitted with ventilation skirts (see 'side rails' p.23), the only sources of draughts will be the door frames. If you only have a door at one end, then you need do nothing further; but if you have a door at each end, you can reduce the flow of air through the tunnel during the cold weather by closing the least-used door permanently for the winter, and packing any substantial gaps between the door and the frame with cloth. This will need to be removed for a good shake-out from time to time to prevent insects from setting up home in it.

75% to 80% of the cost of heating a polytunnel by conventional means is expended at night, when outside temperatures are lowest. Your polytunnel can be equipped with a passive solar heating system simply by providing it with some extra thermal mass: something heavy that stores a lot of heat. This thermal mass absorbs solar energy during the day but takes a long time to release it again at night, and can make a small but important difference to the rate at which the tunnel cools. Probably the easiest way to use thermal mass is to bring some of your water butts into the tunnel for the winter, and fill them. The butts will probably be a dark colour in any case which will make them absorb solar energy well, and, come the warmer weather, the water can be siphoned out to make them easier to remove. Such a system works better in areas with a high proportion of sunny days in winter, since it relies on direct sunlight to work.

For larger tunnels, including a pond in your tunnel is a good way to incorporate thermal mass into the design. Pond plants cope extremely well in tunnel conditions, as do frogs, which will soon colonize it and help out with your slug control, too. As well as acting as a passive solar heater, a pond will also humidify the air in warm conditions.

Another way of providing natural heat is to build a compost heap inside the tunnel within a wooden or straw-bale frame. Although sound in principle, this idea only works if you understand composting sufficiently to keep a heap 'running hot' in the cool conditions of the polytunnel winter, and are able to supply fresh material as needed to keep things ticking over. For most of us the most practical way of doing this is to use partially rotted farmyard manure and straw, with a tarpaulin over the top to make sure that the heap does not give up its heat too quickly. In the spring when the heap is finished, it can be broken down and the compost forked into the top layer of any soil beds, provided it has rotted down thoroughly enough.

It is quite possible to house livestock in a portion of a polytunnel during the winter, provided you prevent them from coming into contact with the cover. Not only will the animals benefit from the warmth and shelter, but their body heat will help to keep night-time temperatures from falling too far. Even chickens can make a substantial difference in this regard; using figures from the College of Agricultural and Environmental Studies at the University of Georgia, a 2.25kg (5 lb) chicken puts out over 50 BTU of heat per hour, or around 14.7 watt hours. This may not seem like a great deal, but even a four-bird coop will contribute as much heat as a 60W incandescent light bulb – useful if you can confine this heat to a cloche tunnel. Please note, however, that a polytunnel is not suitable for housing livestock at other times of the year, as it gets much too hot.

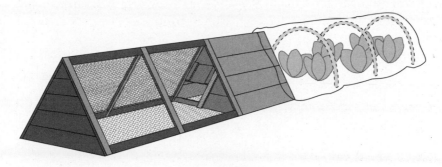

Coop cloche

Some tunnel owners add extra winter insulation to their tunnels by tacking up an extra envelope of industrial bubble wrap, which is recyclable. While this undoubtedly makes a difference, it is tricky and expensive to do, and extremely bulky to store when not in use. Bubble wrap can be used to make an inner tented area which can be heated if absolutely necessary, but a much more practical way is to provide cold frames or fleece mini-tunnels within the body of the main tunnel, and just such a system was pioneered by Eliot Coleman on his farm in Maine (see *Four Season Harvest* detailed in *Further Reading*, p.116, Chelsea Green Publishing, www.chelseagreen.com). He found that although his polytunnel itself did not maintain such high temperatures as an outdoor cold frame during the extremely cold Maine winters, placing a cold frame inside a tunnel conferred very substantial benefits. The diagram below is based on his, but adapted for UK conditions (reproduced with the permission of Chelsea Green Publishing).

Cold frame and tunnel temperatures

Mobile cold frames are easy to make, but for larger areas cloche tunnels (called 'low tunnels' in the US) of horticultural fleece (US: 'floating row cover') are more practical. Horticultural fleece lasts much longer inside a polytunnel than outside because it is not subjected to such rough conditions, and thus a good quality fleece is a very worthwhile investment. Provided it is treated carefully and stored properly when not in use, it will last for many years.

Support hoops for cloche tunnels are available commercially, but you can make oval or rectangular supports yourself from strong wire (at least 3.1mm/9 gauge, available from fencing suppliers) or leftover pieces of plastic water pipe from salvage yards or builders' skips, often for free. These can be spaced every 1.5m (5') and the fabric draped over them and gathered at the ends. Unless the doors at each end are open (an unusual event in winter), there is no wind to disturb the fabric and thus no need to bury the edges in place; a simple length of bamboo cane on top of the excess film on each side will do, but it is still prudent to clip the fabric onto the hoops using clothes pegs or simple metal pipe clips, both of which should last indefinitely. The fabric can be lifted easily for watering or to check for pest activity, but the important point is that it should not touch the plants because it tends to gather condensation during the night. In cold conditions the covers should be replaced immediately after watering or inspection, before they have a chance to freeze to the ground or to themselves.

Hoop and wicket cloches

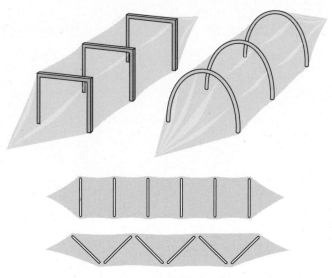

Supports can be placed in a parallel
or diagonal arrangement

In-tunnel cloches

Getting as early a start as possible is important with some hot weather crops such as peppers, which need a slightly longer growing season than we get in the UK. This can be achieved by starting off the plants on south-facing windowsills indoors, by buying the plants from a commercial grower using a heated tunnel (arguably a more efficient use of the heat than many small growers heating their own tunnels, due to scale), or by using a small heated propagator in the tunnel. If you opt for the latter, don't place it on the staging where the lost heat will be wasted; provide it with a dry absorbent surface within one of your cold frames or cloches inside the tunnel, where power needs will be reduced and any wasted heat will benefit neighbouring plants.

A productive, permaculture-led polytunnel

A DIY shade house

Keder house

The hoops in place for a 14' x 20' tunnel

Tunnels need not be ugly

Diagonal bracing on DIY polytunnel

Storm bracing

Tunnel gutter

Early spring planting in new polytunnel

Polytunnels have many uses

The first crops in a new tunnel

Out of season rewards of polytunnel growing

Some organic methods for dealing with pests - see Chapter 7

Suspended shelf

An invaluable extension of a vegetable garden

Chapter 5

Planting Through the Year

The basics of making a planting schedule

A planting schedule is an invaluable tool for getting the most out of your polytunnel, or more specifically the combination of a tunnel and a nearby outdoor plot. To begin with, it's helpful to know which habitat zone you live in. Climatic conditions in the British Isles are quite unique, due to the warmth provided by the Gulf Stream. Nowhere else in the world so far from the equator is as warm in winter, but the summer is correspondingly cool. The plant hardiness zone map of the UK and Ireland, shown below, reflects data collected between 1961 and 2000 by the Irish and UK Met Offices.

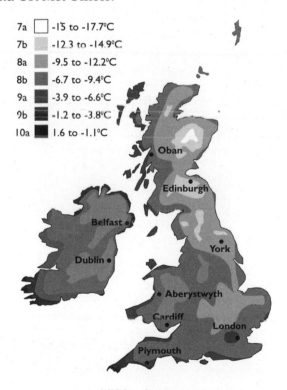

7a	-15 to -17.7°C
7b	-12.3 to -14.9°C
8a	-9.5 to -12.2°C
8b	-6.7 to -9.4°C
9a	-3.9 to -6.6°C
9b	-1.2 to -3.8°C
10a	1.6 to -1.1°C

UK hardiness zones

However, maps like this are only a guide to minimum temperatures outside the tunnel, which of course is the governing factor to what will survive the winter. The greenhouse effect generally provides a one-zone warming effect for the area enclosed by a tunnel, so if you live in zone 8, you will be able to overwinter plants that would otherwise only survive in zone 9. If you use a double-insulated area such as a cloche or cold frame *within* the tunnel, you obtain a further zone of warming, allowing you to grow plants that would normally only survive the winter in zone 10 (see 'Heat'on p.61). This means that someone living in Aberdeen can have winter crops that would otherwise need to be grown in Plymouth.

The most important factor affecting the hardiness of winter planting is protection from the wind, which your tunnel will provide unless you leave the doors at each end fully open on very windy days. After wind effects, the next most important factor is temperature.

The magnitude of heating that a tunnel experiences is proportional to the amount of sunlight that it receives. During the day, even an hour of mid-winter sunshine will see the temperature in a tunnel rocket to 20°C. This is so important that at midwinter, when light levels in the UK are so low that all plant growth has slowed to a crawl, it is still possible to grow many crops in Ohio using a double-skinned tunnel, even though Ohio is much colder. This is because Ohio, being more southerly, receives on average almost 50 percent more sunlight than anywhere in the UK.

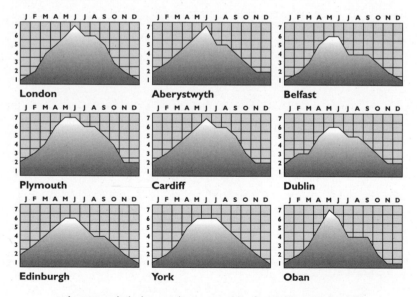

Average daily hours (per month) of sunshine in the UK

In addition to the graphs shown on p.66, listed below is the average number of hours of sunshine per day for the four winter months (November to the end of February), and the same for the four summer months (May to the end of August), for the same nine locations: the greenhouse effect is of most benefit in areas which receive the most sunlight.

	Winter	Summer
London	1.5	5.75
Plymouth	2.25	6.5
Edinburgh	2	5.25
Aberystwyth	2.25	5.75
Cardiff	2.25	6.25
York	1.5	5.75
Belfast	2.5	5
Dublin	2.25	5.5
Kinloss	1.7	5.1
Stornoway	1.4	5.1
Ramsgate	2.2	7.1

Typical hours of sunshine

As well as affecting the temperature of the tunnel, the amount of light getting into the tunnel has a direct effect on the growth of plants. In the UK, low light levels in the winter ensure that, whatever the temperature, nothing grows very much. Rather than struggle against this, the best approach is to treat the tunnel as a holding operation by sowing winter tunnel crops early enough so that their presence through the winter is worthwhile. A full water butt located inside the tunnel will heat up during the day and gradually cool down at night, helping to even out extremes of temperature.

In terms of planning your planting, there are two basic ways in which tunnels can be used. The problem is that they're not compatible, and so a balance must be struck.

A longer season for summer crops

The conventional greenhouse approach, this method takes advantage of the extended growing season a tunnel offers. Planting can start four to six weeks earlier inside the tunnel than outside, and when heat-loving crops such as tomatoes, peppers, aubergine, melon and courgettes come to the end of their productive life outside, plants in the polytunnel will continue to crop for a further month.

A source of food during the winter

The tunnel can be stocked with winter crops such as carrots, lettuce, rocket, radish, winter peas, spinach, chard, beets and Chinese cabbage, and will hold them in a suspended state until light levels increase again in late winter or early spring.

To successfully grow winter crops, you have to have free space in which to transplant them in the autumn. The catch is that if your tunnel is still full of cropping summer plants, you will not have room to start off your winter crops in time. In order to have food throughout the year you have to grow a combination of summer and winter crops, and to do this a well-thought-out planting schedule is essential.

Crop rotation: the pros and cons

Crop rotation is an idea that has been with us for a very long time. It is mentioned in Roman literature, and a cycle of two seasons of growth followed by one of 'fallow' (resting) was used in Europe from the Middle Ages right up until the twentieth century. If some kind of rotation is not practised, the soil quickly becomes depleted to the point where the farmer has to move on. This is the 'slash and burn' method still prevalent in many areas where rainforest runs up against subsistence farming.

Modern crop rotation is usually based on the different nutrient requirements of crops, and in order to combat diseases and pests. For example, in a three-year rotation the nitrogen-hungry brassicas might be grown in plot one, followed by less demanding crops the next year, and crops which are suited to poorer soil (such as the legumes) in year three. At this point compost or manure is added, and the cycle begins again. Perennials, such as asparagus, occupy their own area and are therefore not included.

Mark says:

"Some deviation from the plan is difficult to avoid. For instance, I'm planting leeks in the same bed this year as I used last year. My intention was to have a new bed prepared, but other things – such as writing this book – seem to have got in the way. So I've added some well-rotted manure to help them along. A few years ago I had to plant runner beans in the same place three years in a row in order to avoid shading valuable growing space elsewhere, and I got away with it. But, in general, the garden and the polytunnel should follow a well-defined rotation."

Andy says:

"I had similar problems when I changed my outdoor beds from a four-year rotation to a three-year one, but I was less lucky with my second year of corn, taking casualties from cutworms. While I don't believe in being a slave to rotation, it's the most important defence against soil pests for organic gardeners."

As polytunnels tend to be used to grow intensively, a four-period rotation rather than a three-period one is probably the minimum. The reference here to periods rather than years is because crop rotation in a tunnel can happen much faster than in a garden, as plants are sometimes removed before they have come to the end of their cropping period in order to make room for overwintering crops. When this happens, the replacement plant should belong to the next rotation category regardless of how long the outgoing plant has been there.

In order to define a rotation, crops must be divided into categories. Here's an example of a four-period, category-based rotation:

Period one (hungry): brassicas

Broccoli, Brussels sprouts, cabbage, cauliflower, chinese cabbage, kale, kohlrabi, swede, turnip and radish.

Period two (less hungry): legumes and more

Peas and beans of all kinds, plus chard, lettuce (and other salad vegetables), spinach beet and sweetcorn.

Period three (even less hungry): potatoes and friends

Aubergine, courgette, cucumber, garlic, leek, marrow, onion, pepper, potato, pumpkin, tomato, shallot.

Period four (not hungry): root crops

Beetroot, carrot, parsnip and salsify.

The list can be broken down further to produce a rotation with five or more periods based on vegetable 'families' as well as nutritional needs. In this case the brassicas would be followed by legumes, then onions (including leeks, shallots and garlic), then the potato family (including tomato, aubergine and peppers), and finally the umbellifers such as carrots and parsnips. In this case, the cucumber family (including courgettes, squashes, melons and pumpkins) could be included in the third period as they have similar nutrient requirements to the onion family.

In addition to the value of the rotation itself, it's worth remembering that this system groups similar plants together, making them simpler to care for. For example, all the brassicas are prone to similar pests and may require netting – much easier if they are planted in a group. In a similar way, leaf crops requiring more water can be grouped away from root crops, which generally require less.

The polytunnel as a complement to the vegetable patch

Whatever you can grow in your vegetable patch you can grow it sooner, and probably better, in a tunnel. If there are some crops you wouldn't even attempt to grow in the garden, then try them in the tunnel – with the benefit of shelter and warmth, they may surprise you. At its best, gardening should always have an element of experimentation, and there's nowhere better to try the impossible than in a polytunnel.

A polytunnel can make a wonderful complement to your vegetable patch. If they are used together rather than in isolation, you can extend your harvest in both directions, and enjoy fresh greens and salads right through the winter.

The polytunnel gives protection against three or four degrees of frost, so if you live in hardiness zones 9 or 10 (see p.65) it is likely to remain largely frost-free without any additional protection, but further north it may need some additional help (see 'Heat' in *Life in the Tunnel*). Keeping plants frost-free is obviously better, as some crops – especially the more delicate salad leaves – can't withstand any level of frost at all. Choose your winter varieties with care, and offer additional protection, such as horticultural fleece, for plants that may need it.

The key to how well your tunnel actually complements the rest of your garden depends very much on your intended use. Is the tunnel supposed to extend whatever you're getting from the garden, or to provide something different?

Mark says:

"Last year I had a huge courgette plant in the tunnel, absolutely the biggest I've ever grown (eight separate fruiting branches) which I was loath to cut down even when the garden began supplying more of the same. In the end, I decided that when the garden crop was killed by frost, the tunnel plant would still be growing – and so I left it in place, taking up valuable space which could have been used for winter crops."

Andy says:

"My tunnel produces all sorts of exotics in the summer, but I grow baby carrots in it all year round. That might sound odd, given that they do perfectly well outside, but they take up very little space and grow amazingly quickly. I make a last, large sowing in September, and by the time growing stops I have enough carrots to see the family through the winter – which means that the old carrot bed has had a makeover and now gives us crisp fennel in the autumn instead."

These are the kinds of decision a tunnel owner has to take on a regular basis.

If you really want your tunnel to provide winter crops, you need to be ruthless enough to cut down productive plants to make room for those, which will see you through the long, dim months when only the hardiest of crops will be coming out of the garden. Winter crops need to be in by the end of August, or September at the very latest. Only then will they be mature enough by the time the slow- or no-growth period hits.

In most areas, winter crops can be started in pots or modules in the tunnel early enough to be well established by the time the summer crop plants are removed. Legumes will also tolerate being undersown during the same period; this is the practice of planting them under and around the existing summer crops and watering well. The seeds will germinate but not grow strongly due to lack of light, and will be ready to grow away as soon as the summer crops are removed. Undersowing requires great care to be taken when the summer planting is removed, as it's easy to wreck everything during the removal process. Cutting the outgoing plants off just below ground level can be a better alternative to pulling them out, although pests (such as underground slugs) may be attracted while the roots rot down.

Another factor to bear in mind regarding the timing of winter crops is the 'hungry gap' between the end of winter and the first of the new season crops. This is the thinnest time of year for kitchen gardeners, when nothing much is available in the outdoor plot other than early-sprouting broccoli, kale and leeks, augmented by stored onions, root crops and the like. In the tunnel, and especially if you introduce the additional insulation provided by a cloche or cold frame, you can meet this challenge by getting a very early start on lettuce, radish, spinach, rocket and a host of other leaf vegetables – all of which will make a very welcome change in the kitchen. February-planted early potatoes will be ready around the end of April and, if you timed it right, summer-planted tunnel cauliflower will come in just as you need it.

Mark says:

"My own tunnel is a combination of perennial and annual plantings and so, obviously enough, the perennial areas remain constant through the year (incidentally, here in Wales we harvested globe artichokes in January). What ends up being planted in the annual area depends on both my outdoor plan and what I'd like to grow in the coming winter."

Andy says:

"Although I clear most of my tunnel out for winter plantings, some crops like peppers are just too good to root out early. I use a combination of module starts and undersowing to get winter plants going in time, but I also grow some early crops, like corn and strawberries. I could of course use day-neutral strawberries to keep going until December, but in the tunnel I just use runners from my ordinary plants. These fruit a few weeks sooner than the ones outside, and are finished in plenty of time to make a clear space for winter crops."

Planting plans and local conditions vary hugely, but here is a general list of what might be happening in your tunnel, season by season.

Winter

Crop

Celeriac, celery, lettuce, rocket, corn salad, spring onion, overwintering beet, carrot, chard, chicory, endive, escarole, kohlrabi, mizuna, parsley, radicchio, radish, sorrel, turnip. Enjoy the last of any summer crops you might have had room to keep, such as courgettes and sweet peppers. Primocaine ('everbearing' or 'autumn') raspberries and day-neutral strawberries will continue to crop until temperatures really fall.

Tasks

Remove any plant debris. As soil becomes vacant, top-dress with 7.5cm (3") of compost. Prepare tender plants for the coldest weather and bring tender plants into the tunnel for overwintering. Ensure you have a decent supply of tunnel repair tape, just in case. Chit early potatoes and put together your planting schedule for the coming year.

Spring

Sow

Plant the summer crops such as aubergines, tomatoes, peppers, cour-gettes, cucumbers, melons and early onion starts. Also sow French and runner beans, celery, sweetcorn, tomatoes and cauliflowers in pots or modules for later planting out in the vegetable garden. Start hanging-basket and bedding plants. Sow the first salad plants of the year: lettuce, coriander, radish, rocket, chard, etc. A continual succession of these and other plants throughout the year can be obtained by further small sow-ings every few weeks until growth stops in the winter.

Crop

Globe artichokes, autumn-planted peas and broad beans, radishes, pars-ley, spinach, chard, salsify, early potatoes, endive, scorzonera, rhubarb, strawberries. Winter salad plants will start to grow again, then bolt as light levels increase. With regular cropping of leaves and pinching out of flowering stems, harvesting can be prolonged until new plantings become ready.

Tasks

Open the tunnel for no less than an hour a day except on the coldest days, but be careful to close it at least an hour before sunset. Be prepared to use horticultural fleece to protect delicate seedlings from low temperatures, and also as a sunscreen. Clean the cover and exposed surfaces as detailed on pp.30-31. Clear out all plant debris and remove unused pots etc.

Summer

Sow

Bulb fennel (in modules, as they don't transplant well), Chinese cabbage, chard, spring cabbage. Sow sweetcorn direct into the soil for a late crop.

Broccoli, peas and more French beans can be started for later transplanting outside. Continue successional sowing of salad leaves.

Crop

Elephant garlic, courgettes, cucumbers, sweet and chilli peppers (taken green), aubergines, melons, tomatoes, basil, sweetcorn, watermelon, primocaine raspberries and exotics (see p.109). Don't let early sowings of salad get away from you – keep on top of eating the young plants and be ruthless with composting anything that gets past its best.

Tasks

If the tunnel needs to be re-covered, this is the time of year to do it. Keep doors open from early morning until sunset. Plant up hanging baskets. Give extra water (and feed, if necessary) to fast-growing plants like tomatoes and the squash family. Every other day, check these fast-growing plants are securely tied up and remove all unwanted side shoots. Tap or mist tomato plants daily for better pollination.

Autumn

Sow

Tunnel winter crops need to be sown by the end of September at the very latest. Here are some potential winter tunnel crops to consider, which are all likely to survive right through until spring: celery, chard, chicory, Chinese cabbage, carrots, cauliflowers, corn salad, beetroots, endive, lettuces (all kinds), mizuna, winter peas, parsley, autumn-sown broad beans, radishes, rocket and spinach.

Crop

Globe artichokes (second flowering), peppers and chilli peppers (taken red), tomatoes, basil, physalis, melons, watermelons, cucumbers, courgettes, aubergines, celeriac (does well with longer growing season), celery, fennel, primocaine raspberries, monster-sized onions, French and runner beans. Pumpkins should be brought in and left for 7-10 days to cure the skins; onions dry well on the staging and can be stored over winter in strings hanging from the crop bars.

Tasks

Inspect the entire tunnel cover, and fix anything that flaps by using repair tape on both sides of the cover. Clear away summer crops to make way for winter planting and clip up unwanted string supports with clothes pegs. Keep the doors open all day and keep a close eye out for moulds and fungi, especially on blight-prone plants such as tomatoes – which should have their tops nipped out towards the end of September to prevent any more fruit trusses from forming. Top-dress bare soil with compost. Bring pot-grown herbs such as basil into the tunnel to extend their season. If your local climate is too cool to do so outside, some early potatoes can be planted in soil beds or deep pots to provide a crop of new potatoes for the table at Christmas.

Chapter 6

Preventing Pests

The value of prompt action: everything grows faster in a tunnel

Gardening in a polytunnel requires continual vigilance against pests. Any polytunnel becomes a trap for hundreds of insects throughout the year, and anyone who has gardened under plastic knows that once something gets in, it's difficult for it to find its way out again – so you can imagine how hard it can be to get rid of insects that, once inside, find the food plant of their dreams living there.

The case against poisons

Humans have applied pesticides to protect their crops for thousands of years. There is evidence of elemental sulphur dusting in Sumeria as early as 4,500 years ago, probably to control the growth of moulds and fungi. Such treatments are relatively benign, but as human knowledge of chemistry advanced so did our use of increasingly poisonous compounds such as lead and mercury. The single biggest advance in our knowledge of pesticides, however, was arguably the discovery of the effectiveness of DDT as an insecticide by Paul Müller in 1939, which quickly became the most widely used pesticide in the world. It wasn't until the late 1950s that serious questions about its safety and environmental effects were raised.

These days it is recognized that DDT (and its breakdown products DDE and DDD) are toxic to a wide range of organisms, particularly birds and aquatic life, and they have been linked to cancer[1] and reproductive disorders[2] in humans. DDT was finally banned in most developed countries in the 1970s and 1980s, but it is so persistent in the environment that in 2005, 33 years after the implementation of a ban in the USA, 85% of milk samples tested by the US Department of Agriculture still had detectable levels of DDE.[3] With the well-being of governments and global agribusiness positively dependent on the use of pesticides for intensive farming, the pattern set by DDT – that of rapid uptake followed by the later emergence of safety concerns – is sadly typical of pesticides.

Across the EEC at the end of July 2003, 81 pesticides and weed-killers were withdrawn from legal sale despite having been previously declared 'safe'. A degree of cynicism would seem to be the only sensible approach to manufacturers' safety claims. Pesticides, fungicides and herbicides, whether organic or chemical, should always be treated as the last resort – especially in a polytunnel, where they won't be washed away as they might be elsewhere in the garden. Chemicals may leave hazardous residues in the soil or vegetation, and both chemical and organic controls commonly affect many more species than those at which they are aimed. They can result in a serious imbalance, possibly lasting for years, in what would otherwise be healthy soil.

Mark says:

"By using sacrificial plants and removing slugs, caterpillars etc. I am able to grow vegetables and flowers organically, without deliberately killing anything. It's a bit more work, but not much. I believe this benefits me as well as other living things.

"As a practising Buddhist for over 30 years, I am convinced that killing is not an approach worth considering anywhere or any time, and that includes the garden. Accordingly I remove or discourage pests and accept, indeed anticipate, a certain degree of loss. This attitude has never been a problem for me, and while gardening may take me a little more time, I don't find that to be a problem either – quite the opposite, in fact. I know that my garden is a safe haven for all who travel within it, despite the loss of an occasional plant."

Andy says:

"I regard having to use a pesticide as a failure on my part – a failure to provide the right environment, to give a plant a good start, or to act quickly enough at the first sign of trouble. Although I will, reluctantly and as a last resort, use an organic pesticide if things get out of hand elsewhere in the garden, I no longer do so in the tunnel. The more I learn, the less happy about pesticides I become."

Pesticides

Slug pellets

Slug pellets usually contain metaldehyde or methiocarb. The manufacturers claim that these are not harmful to other species 'if used properly', and include blue colourings or bittering agents in an attempt to repel other animals. However, metaldehyde is poisonous to mammals and can damage or kill a wide variety of other useful garden animals, especially birds (which are likely to be regular visitors to your tunnel, unless you deliberately exclude them). This is hardly surprising, as the basic material used to make the pellets is grain (the same as for dry dog food); the UK Ministry of Agriculture once suggested the use of slug pellets as a means of controlling small mammals on farms.[4]

Methiocarb is approximately ten times more poisonous than metaldehyde, and not only kills slugs but is a powerful insecticide, therefore killing a much wider range of species – including beetle species which act as important allies in controlling slugs in the tunnel, by eating their eggs and hatchlings.

Deltamethrin

Deltamethrin is a synthetic version of a chemical named pyrethrin which is extracted from chrysanthemums. It has been engineered to be more toxic than pyrethrin, and to take longer to break down. It is often combined with other compounds, which increase its potency and compromise the human body's ability to eliminate it. It is toxic to all insects and has been linked to human fatalities due to respiratory failure, as well as being implicated in increases in rates of breast cancer. It is also highly toxic to a wide variety of marine life when present at concentrations as low as one part per billion.

Roundup

Roundup is possibly the most commonly used herbicide available today. While conventional wisdom considers it to be a generally safe product, there are valid concerns regarding its use. Roundup's main ingredient, glyphosate, is classed as 'dangerous for the environment' and 'toxic for aquatic organisms' by the European Union.[5] Its use also leads to an increase in the disease rate in the following crop, indicating damage to soil flora.[6]

Monsanto, Roundup's manufacturer, claims that Roundup fully degrades in the soil by microbial action, leaving no harmful residues. However, in the light of recent court proceedings in France where this claim has been refuted, a degree of caution may be appropriate.

Moreover, many states in the USA and elsewhere now report the presence of glyphosate-resistant weeds.[7,8]

Pyrethrum

A low-toxicity insecticide originally made from the powdered flowers of certain species of chrysanthemum, pyrethrum's first use on a grand scale was probably when it was employed by Napoleon's armies to combat lice and fleas. It has since been used as a 'natural' control of many species of garden pest, but it is shockingly non-selective. The label on a pyrethrum-based insecticide manufactured in Fresno, California, says that it will kill "Ants, Aphids, Armyworms, Asparagus Beetle, Blister Beetles, Cabbage Looper, Caterpillars, Cockroaches, 12-spotted Cucumber Beetle, Colorado Potato Beetles, Corn Earworm, Crickets, Cross-striped Cabbageworm, Cucumber Beetles, Deer Fly, Diamondback Larvae, Fireworms, Flea Beetles, Fruit Flies, Fruit Tree Leafroller, Grape Leafhopper, Green Peach Aphids, Greenhouse Thrips, Gypsy Moth (adults & larvae), Harlequin Bug, Heliothis, Imported Cabbageworm, Leafhopper, Leafrollers, Leaftiers, Lice, Mexican Bean Beetle, Potato Leafhopper, Psyllids, Skippers, Stink Bugs, Thrips, Vinegar Flies, Webworms and Whiteflies."

Pyrethrum kills species that are beneficial to gardens and polytunnels with the same efficacy that it kills pests. It breaks down rapidly in sunlight, but is highly toxic to fish and other aquatic species, such as visiting frogs and toads, whilst active.

Copper mixtures

There are several copper compounds available for use in gardens as fungicides or bactericides. Copper hydroxide and copper sulphate are both considered to be level 1 toxicity ('danger') by the US-EPA, but nevertheless both are allowed as organic controls in the USA. In the UK, copper sulphate is usually applied as Bordeaux mixture where it is combined with calcium hydroxide (hydrated lime).

Copper compounds typically remain on the leaf surface for between 1 and 2 weeks or until washed off by overhead irrigation. Because it is a highly 'binding' metal, it tends to remain in the soil in all but sandy environments, and even outside it can eventually build up to toxic levels if it is repeatedly applied. In high concentrations, horticultural copper compounds are poisonous to bees and earthworms, and long-term exposure to low levels of copper have been linked to anaemia and liver disease in humans.

Diatomaceous earth

Diatomaceous earth consists of the fossilized remains of diatoms, a type of hard-shelled algae, crushed into a fine white powder. It acts as an insecticide by absorbing lipids from the outer layer of insects' exoskeleton, causing death by dehydration. Slugs and snails dislike it too.

The main problem is that diatomaceous earth is utterly non-selective, killing all insects indiscriminately – including beneficial species such as rove beetles and visiting bees. In the confined space of a tunnel, repeated or heavy use of diatomaceous earth may result in it building up to the point where it begins to kill all insects, including beneficial ones, as it is slow to break down. Its use in the tunnel is therefore not recommended except as a final resort.

Insecticidal soap

Used to control soft-bodied pests such as aphids and thrips, insecticidal soaps are sprayed onto the affected plant. Typically they have a low degree of toxicity, and are therefore very unlikely to affect mammals. However, plants may be damaged – so test-spray a small area before treating your entire crop. If yellow or brown spots appear on the leaves over the next couple of days, you should probably switch to a different control method.

Usually the concentration of soap to water is around 2%. You can make your own by adding a couple of tablespoons of phosphate-free dish detergent (look for 'safe for septic tanks' on the label) to a gallon of water. When a small amount of a vegetable oil (cooking or olive oil, for example) is added to the mix its 'sticking power' increases and it becomes somewhat effective against powdery mildew.

Sodium bicarbonate (and potassium bicarbonate)

Sodium bicarbonate, also known as bicarbonate of soda and baking soda, is mixed with water to produce a fungicidal spray that can be helpful in preventing the spread of powdery mildew. Both these chemicals have been rated with a toxicity level 3 ('caution') by the US/EPA – despite the fact that baking soda has been used as a foodstuff for hundreds of years. Bicarbonate-based fungicides are not approved for market in the UK, but a household fungicide spray can easily be made by dissolving 10g (2 level teaspoonfuls) of food-grade sodium bicarbonate in a litre (quart) of water, and adding a couple of drops of phosphate-free dish detergent to improve its wetting properties. Potassium bicarbonate is more effective if you can get it. The amount of sodium that ends up in the soil when using a spray like this is not significant, but even so prevention is always the watchword with fungal infections of any kind.

Sulphur

Sulphur sprays and dusts are used to deal with scab, powdery mildew and mites, and can also be used to lower soil pH. A naturally occurring chemical, it is considered to be an organic control. As a mildew control, dust it over the affected leaves when they are dry, but remember to wash any produce thoroughly before use.

Biocontrols

As shall be seen later in this chapter, aphids can reproduce at a frightening rate, even in the absence of a mate; yet we are not knee-deep in aphids. The reason for this is that aphids are constantly being preyed upon by a wide variety of predators and diseases, so that the ecosystem as a whole remains stable. This process is known as biocontrol.

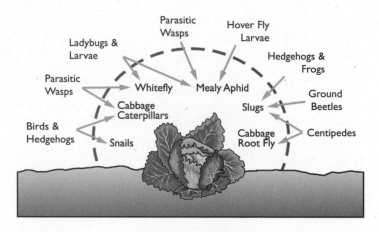

Predators and pests

Commercial biocontrols are a relatively new option for gardeners. Packs of various predator larvae, disease spores, parasitic nematodes and suchlike are available for application to the growing area, and produce a gratifying crash in the populations of target species. However, biocontrol need not always mean paying for a quick fix from the garden centre; with some planning it is possible to use the sophisticated web of biocontrols that already exists in your area to help control pest numbers. Examples of these might include planting a patch of poached egg plant near your tunnel to attract hover-flies, important aphid predators that might go on to snack on the pests in your tunnel, or providing a toad habitat nearby such as a pile of untreated rotting wood so that toads might be tempted to visit the tunnel in search of slugs.

When using any biocontrol it is very important to consider the wider implications of bringing in an organism that is not already present in your local ecosystem. Harlequin ladybirds (multicoloured ladybugs, *Harmonia axyridis*) were introduced from Asia to North America in an attempt to control aphids, and recently appeared in the UK. The harlequins are very effective at aphid control, but when food supplies run low, they turn on butterflies, lacewings and native ladybirds, as well as causing damage to soft fruit and becoming a pest in human dwellings as they seek to hibernate in winter.

Netting, fleecing and sacrificial plants

Covering plants with netting avoids difficult situations such as caterpillar infestations. When covering brassicas, make sure that there is a gap between the netting and the plants themselves by using some form of support, or butterflies will lay their eggs on leaves that they can reach through the netting. When dealing with birds there is no need to create a gap, and netting can just be thrown over blackberry bushes etc. to prevent crop loss.

Crops such as beans and peas, which pests may dig up immediately after planting, can also be netted directly on the soil surface until they have germinated. Netting may be preferable to fleece, as you can see through it to the emerging seedling without needing to move it out of the way.

Fruit cages are large, walk-in frameworks entirely enclosed in netting that deny birds access to your soft fruit area. This is also possible within the confines of a polytunnel by adding net curtains at either end, weighted at the bottom to stop the wind from blowing them about. Birds are not usually a problem in polytunnels because only small birds are manoeuvrable enough to fly in and out with ease, but using a smaller mesh size will exclude butterflies and this is where net curtains really come into their own. This may not be such a good idea if you are growing crops that rely on insect pollination, such as early strawberries. Although in practice enough insects still gain access, it may be necessary to leave the curtains open for short periods under supervision, or to resort to hand pollination.

NOTE: On very windy sites curtains may be ineffective, and screen doors may be a better option.

As well as providing protection against frost, garden fleece is extremely helpful in denying pests access to young plants. It also prevents the soil surface from drying out so quickly, which is especially useful when germinating carrots and other tiny seeds after the weather has begun to warm. Unlike mulch, which also prevents the soil drying out, a fleece can be lifted out of the way so that slugs and other pests can be easily removed.

'Sacrificial plant' is a term given to anything planted deliberately to keep pests away from your valuable crops. These can be plants that are more attractive to them than the crop plants, such as nasturtiums for aphids, or plants which you don't mind losing, such as an extra brassica or two onto which caterpillars can be relocated.

A quarantine area

Introducing new plants into your garden always carries a risk of introducing pests and diseases. Garden centres and other commercial sources have a professional interest in making sure that their plants are healthy and vigorous, and will do their best to ensure that pests and diseases don't get a foothold. Plants given to you by well-meaning friends and neighbours have a much higher risk, since they may not be experienced enough to know when they have trouble brewing.

When dealing with any new plant, but especially those donated by friends or neighbours, it is important to establish a quarantine area where they can be kept for observation before introducing them to the tunnel environment. A cold frame or small greenhouse is ideal for this, but a sunny windowsill will do.

Keep a careful eye on quarantined plants for pests that are difficult to spot. Spider mite, for example, can live on a plant for some time before symptoms of its presence are clearly visible; don't move the plants into the tunnel until you're sure that they are healthy.

Mould growth and tunnel hygiene

Moulds are a fact of life in a polytunnel, as they are with growing under any sort of cover. You are unlikely to ever completely get rid of them, but you can control them, most of the time.

Good housekeeping is essential to prevent mould. Always keep the tunnel clear of debris of all kinds, and provide good ventilation to control humidity. Even on cool, damp days, get the doors at least part way open early in the morning. The earlier this can happen, the sooner the overnight condensation can dry out. This is especially important during autumn, when the air tends to be damp and has high circulating levels of fungal spores.

Avoid crowded planting, as this decreases air circulation and allows moulds and mildews to spread very rapidly.

Once or twice a year, or more often in damp climates, use a damp sponge to clean the inside of the cover to remove residues of algae and mould. This can be done as part of your regular maintenance cleaning of the outside of the tunnel (see pp.30-31). Be careful doing this when your cover is over three years old, as it won't be as elastic as it used to be. Covers should last for at least five years if treated carefully, but they do become brittle with age.

As every tunnel owner knows, many insects will fly in and then be unable to fly out again, as they tend to fly upwards in order to try to escape. This means that many of them will fall to the ground and die, and then decompose, creating another focus for mould growth. Screen doors and mesh curtains will allow ventilation while helping to keep insects out.

It's possible to fold the cover into pleats around the door frame in two ways: one with the 'pocket' on the inside, and one with it on the outside. Either way, the pockets will fill with water – from rain, or from condensation. Bugs will fall into them, die, and decompose – leading to potential mould problems. To avoid this, make sure you fold the cover in such a way that any pockets formed remain on the outside of the tunnel (see pp.42-3).

Botrytis

Botrytis is a common disease affecting a variety of plants both inside and out, but predominantly in greenhousing. Polytunnels are even more vulnerable because of their tendency towards condensation. The first stage causes brown spots to appear on the leaves, which are quickly followed by patches of grey mould. If left to itself, botrytis can infect an entire crop in a matter of days. In a polytunnel the most commonly affected plants are tomatoes, with potatoes (usually an outdoor crop) close behind. Plants which do well in full sun such as cucumbers, squashes, peppers etc. are more prone to botrytis than others, and shouldn't be planted in shady or damp spots.

There are currently no fungicides available to home gardeners for the specific control of botrytis. You can spray affected plants with Bordeaux mixture, which contains copper sulphate and so is not strictly an 'organic' approach, but the problem with copper is that even outside a tunnel it is very persistent in soil and can build up to toxic levels. Its use in polytunnels is therefore not recommended. Potassium or sodium bicarbonate spray is an alternative that can be effective (see p.81).

The key to botrytis management, as with all moulds, is prevention rather than cure. The best way to achieve this is, once again, to ensure there is good air circulation around your plants and to keep a close eye on them, especially in damp conditions. Know what to look out for, and remove affected leaves at the first sign of trouble. In the case of indeterminate tomatoes, nip out all unwanted sideshoots to avoid creating a dense bush which would impede airflow. If any sideshoots manage to escape your attention until they're 10-15cm (4"-6") long, you can plant these in compost where they will readily take root, making more tomato plants. On a more general note, it is important to keep the tunnel free of dead and decaying material at all times, as this is a likely source of mould spores.

Potato blight

Potato blight, which also affects tomatoes, is caused by a primitive fungus-like organism named *Phytophthora infestans*. It is spread by wind and rain under warm, humid conditions, but its most likely route into your poly-tunnel is on infected seed potatoes or tomato plants, or on the soles of your shoes if you have the infection elsewhere in the garden. The first symptoms are brown or black areas appearing on the leaves, with a white bloom developing on the underside of leaves as they die. It spreads very quickly to all parts of the plant above ground.

If left unchecked, blight will quickly move down the plant and into the roots and tubers, so at the first sign of the disease cut down all the vegetation to ground level and burn it to destroy the spores. Harvest the entire crop roughly three weeks later, keeping a close eye on the crop in storage. Management of the disease outside the tunnel is the same, but it is very easy to carry spores into the tunnel if you have been handling or walking on infected material. Therefore if you have been dealing with blight outside the tunnel, it will be necessary to change and launder your clothes, and rinse off your footwear, before going back into the tunnel. If any affected potatoes are accidentally left to grow the following year, they may become 'primary infectors' and quickly cause another outbreak.

Avoidance of blight is very important in cool, damp summers. Always buy fresh commercial seed potatoes, which are monitored for the disease, and always water around the base of plants rather than spraying the leaves, as moulds prefer damp conditions.

Mildew

Generally, mildews prosper in still, humid air and appear as a white powdery bloom, typically on the upper side of plant leaves. Increase the circulation of air in your tunnel, especially where mildew-prone crops are growing; these include tomato, cucumber and the other squashes, and calendula – a flower often grown near crops to attract insects. Although the cause is a different organism, the prevention and treatment of mildew is very similar to that of botrytis (see above).

Herbs as an alternative to pesticides

Interplanting a vegetable garden with herbs is an attractive and beneficial way of confusing or discouraging pests that are guided by scent. Some of them, especially the aromatics such as thyme, marjoram and mint, will also attract bees and hover-flies, which will pollinate other plants (although less so if you are using screen doors or mesh curtains). Hover-flies are also voracious aphid predators.

Plants that can help keep pests away

Basil – flies and mosquitoes.
Catnip – flea beetles (but not to be used in areas where cats are present, unless you want everything squashed).
Horseradish – potato bugs.
Mint – 'cabbage white' butterflies (which are actually several different species) and ants.
Marigold – asparagus beetles and tomato worm.
Rosemary – bean beetles and carrot flies.
Sage – white butterflies and carrot flies.
Thyme – cabbage worms.
Wormwood – deters animals from garden.

You may also consider planting sacrificial plants such as nasturtium, tansy and impatiens to which aphids will be attracted in preference to valuable crop plants.

Make your cover work for you

Some polytunnel covers can actually help to reduce infestations of many pests, including aphids, by blocking out some or all of the UV (ultraviolet) light. As flying insects need ultraviolet to track their target plants, without it they don't fly. While aphids may still form small colonies, in a UV-screened tunnel they will not spread rapidly, and so the need for chemical or biocontrols is reduced. Diseases such as botrytis and mildew require UV light in order to release their spores, and so their spread is also slowed.

Dealing with pests: the Rogue's Gallery

Ants

Ants are generally bad news in the tunnel, which unfortunately provides them with an ideal environment. They love warm, dry conditions and will bring eggs and developing pupae to just below the surface, some-times under a stone, for additional warmth. Not only do they make nests which can undermine plants, causing them to wilt or die, but they steal small seeds from pots and soil beds, taking them back to the nest for the protein. They also 'farm' aphids, stroking them with their antennae to persuade them to release droplets of a sweet sap, which they collect and take back to the nest. Any other insect that may be a predator to 'their' aphids is likely to be killed. Ants are predators, and so their presence is not always a problem. When they need to be discouraged, they are extremely difficult to remove.

One method of eradicating a complete nest is to lay a bait of sugar solution into which some borax has been mixed. Provided a removable bait station such as a coin with a plant saucer over it is used, borax is accepted as an organic solution because it is a naturally occurring min-eral and the amounts used are tiny. If fresh bait is put down each evening the ants will collect it and take it back to the nest where it will kill the whole colony, but this is only completely effective when ants are actively seeking sugar, typically in spring and early summer. It is much less effec-tive at other times of the year.

Digging out an ant nest is a drastic measure which is also likely to damage surrounding plants, and unlikely to be effective unless a very large amount of earth is removed. Sometimes a nest can be persuaded to relocate by repeated flooding of the area with cold water, but it may only move a short distance away. Boiling water is sometimes used, but you have to know exactly where the brood chambers are for this to work, and the hot water kills everything indiscriminately, causing untold damage to the ecosystem present in a fertile, balanced soil. If you must kill the nest, a commercial nematode-based biological control may be your only option.

The other option for dealing with ants is to defend particular plants. If ants are seen climbing up and down a particular plant it is probably because they are farming the aphids on it. A sticky ring of grease, non-drying glue, or petroleum jelly placed around the stem of plants or in a ring around the outside of pots will deny access. Ants cannot cross water with detergent in it, so particular pots can also be defended by placing them on a brick surrounded by a 'moat' of soapy water.

According to manufacturers, ants can sometimes be repelled using small, commercially available generators of either a combination of electromagnetic pulses and ultrasonic sound waves, or just ultrasonic sound waves. Unfortunately there seems to be very little evidence that these devices work against ants, and therefore they cannot be recommended.

Aphids

While there are many different species of aphid, most can only live on a small number of plant species. Aphids are sap-sucking insects, and will attack all exposed parts of a plant including the roots. They tend to congregate on soft, young growth, and when their numbers build up they cause new growth to become weak and distorted. Badly affected plants may be killed outright, especially when young. To make things worse, aphids can spread viruses from plant to plant as they fly and feed, and are often deliberately farmed by ants (see the entry for 'Ants' above for how to deal with this).

While specifics differ between species, the following numbers are a reasonably accurate guide: a newborn aphid becomes a reproducing adult at the age of 1 week, and can then produce up to 5 offspring per day for up to 30 days. They can reproduce asexually, i.e. without the presence of a male. So, let's say one adult aphid enters your tunnel and finds a suitable host plant. One week later, there are 35 aphids – a small clump. A week after that, there are 70 – but it's what happens next that should alarm the tunnel-keeper. By the end of the third week there are another 35 aphids from the original invader, but the aphids she gave birth to in the first week are now mature and have each given birth to 35 more – a total of 1,225. The primary colony has now split up into many smaller colonies, and the situation is out of control. If everything went the aphids' way, there would be a staggering 1,590,155 of them by the time the first one reached the end of her reproductive life, at the beginning of the fifth week.

In practice, things aren't that bad. These numbers assume a 'zero' death rate from predation and disease and an infinite food supply, but it's by no means uncommon for the aphid population on an affected crop to double every two days; so they are a very serious pest – especially in a polytunnel.

The Oregon State University in the US has done a lot of research on aphids, and recommends the use of insecticidal soaps rather than conventional insecticides. However, in the US, the EPA found that while the toxicity of insecticidal soaps is generally low, they have caused genetic damage and birth defects in laboratory tests and are also highly toxic to aquatic animals.

Odd as it may sound, the most important thing that you can do to prevent aphids from becoming a problem is not to use insecticides anywhere near the tunnel. If no insecticides are used, the predator numbers exist in balance with the aphids and so they are rarely a problem, except in late winter and early spring when constant vigilance is required.

If an infestation does occur, remove the affected leaves where possible. If it's a serious infestation, consider removing the entire plant. Squishing the aphids by hand can be effective if there are not many of them, but take care in any of these actions as some aphids may be startled into flight. Since the insects are less active at low temperatures, this can be minimized by lifting plants early in the morning, before the sun is on the tunnel. Covering crops with a fleece is an effective preventative measure against many pests, including aphids; so covering 'clean' plants of the same type can help prevent the spread of an infestation.

There are other things that you can change in the tunnel to make infestation less likely; avoid over-fertilizing susceptible plants, since aphids are attracted to soft, sappy growth; use sacrificial plants such as nasturtiums in pots which can be readily moved out of the tunnel along with the invaders; attract predators such as hover-flies and lacewings by interplanting with *Tagetes* or *Asteraceae* (daisy) species. Pot marigolds and the poached egg plant (*Limnanthes douglasii*) are popular choices.

Another important aphid predator is the ladybird (ladybug). These will usually find your garden and a lot of the aphids in it, but the eggs can also be purchased as biocontrols.

NOTE: *If buying online, be sure that you purchase a species that already exists locally. Introduced species can outcompete and displace native ones and become pests in their own right. Ladybird larvae are particularly voracious, and just two or three individuals drafted from elsewhere in the garden can make a big dent in the aphid population of your tunnel.*

Other biocontrols available include *Aphidoletes*, a midge predatory to aphids, and *Aphidius*, a tiny parasitic wasp native to North America. Their use in a confined space will be more effective than out in the open. It is worthwhile being aphid-aware when placing your annual seed order – there are varieties of plants available which are partially resistant to aphids and the viruses that they carry.

If things spiral out of control and drastic action is called for, there are aphid-killing sprays based on rapeseed and other plant oils available through organic gardening stores which will only kill what they hit, and are harmless to larger insects such as bees, lacewings and ladybirds. Aphids can also be sprayed from plants using a strong jet of cold water. As this is not usually 100% effective it will need to be repeated, so evaluate the situation beforehand. Aphids love lush, tender growth and tend to congregate around the softer growing tips, which are more prone to damage by a jet of water than elsewhere.

Andy says:

> "Spraying aphids off plants with a jet of water works really well provided you can get the spray right – you need a small jet of water under quite a bit of pressure."

Cabbage root flies

Cabbage root fly is almost never a problem in polytunnels, as the insects seem to find it impossible to home in on their host plant. However, if you are unfortunate enough to see this pest, it is easily prevented in future years by placing a protective collar around the base of each cabbage seedling as it is planted out, or by growing the plant under fleece from the very beginning.

You can purchase collars or make your own: cut out a piece of plain brown (i.e. unbleached) cardboard about 20cm across, then cut a slit from the edge to the centre. You'll also need to create a small hole there, about the width of a pencil, to accommodate the seedling stem. Cardboard will work for a while but is likely to need replacing at some point during the season, while commercially-produced 'cabbage stem guards' that will last the entire season are available at garden centres.

Carrot flies

Carrot fly doesn't only affect carrots, as its name suggests; parsnips, parsley and celery are also prone to damage. Happily, as for cabbage root fly, tunnel use seems to confer almost total protection from this pest.

However, if you live in an area prone to fly damage, it might be better to take some precautions. If carrots are sown in late May (June in the north) they will be too late to be affected by the first generation of eggs. If harvested in early August, they avoid the second. A winter crop can then be sown after the end of August. Plant thinly, as the fly is attracted by the scent of bruised carrot leaves. Outdoor trials have shown that the damage caused by carrot fly is reduced by interplanting with a strongly-scented crop such as onion or garlic, although quite a lot of this is needed; the effect could be replicated in a polytunnel by planting a patch of garlic on the leeward (sheltered) side of the tunnel. Alternatively, a carrot crop grown under horticultural fleece will be entirely protected from this pest.

Caterpillars

Pesticides and biocontrols are not species-specific and will act against any caterpillars they contact. This should be considered, especially as many British butterfly species are endangered. The so-called 'Cabbage White' actually includes several different species, and white butterflies in general include some of our most common as well as our rareset butterflies, including the Black-Veined White, which became extinct in Britain around 1925.

There are also several biological controls available: *Steinernema carpcapse*, a nematode which attacks the caterpillars; *Bacillus thuringiensis*, which also kills them, but is non-specific and will also kill other species; and the trichogramma wasp, a tiny parasitic insect that lays its eggs on the caterpillars. However, it is very simple to prevent infestation by covering the plants with fleece or netting before the butterflies lay eggs on them, or by protecting the entire tunnel with screen doors or mesh curtains. If this is not possible, caterpillars can be picked off by hand and relocated to a sacrificial plant (nasturtiums, or any spare brassica seedlings) outside the tunnel. If they're too small to pick up easily, use a small, soft paintbrush, or wait a few days until they're bigger, when they can be picked up with less risk of harm. Crushing caterpillars on the plant is a bad idea, since the decaying debris increases the risk of fungal disease.

Cats and chickens

Although chickens may not be a specific problem in urban areas, cats are fairly ubiquitous and need no introduction. Cats appreciate the warmth and the calm of a tunnel environment and may well decide to set up a regular nest in a leafy bed, whereas chickens and other poultry are likely to scratch up plants in search of bugs and worms. Cats are particularly fond of hiding if they don't want to be ejected, and are perfectly capable of shredding their way through the cover if it occurs to them to do so. If either of these animals causes havoc in the tunnel, the simplest and surest way to deal with them is to introduce an inner door or gate of wide mesh which is kept closed at all times. If this is not an attractive option, particular areas of a tunnel can be defended from cats by top-dressing the soil with a mulch of chopped holly leaves, which cats will not walk over.

Clubroot

All brassicas are prone to this disease, spread by a soil-borne fungus that causes thick, distorted roots and leads to stunted plants and reduced harvest. Unfortunately, there is no known cure. Fortunately, some varieties are resistant. Plants grown in pots are unlikely to be affected, and good crop rotation plus the addition of lime, up to a pH of around 7 or 7.5, will help to prevent the disease.

Cutworms

Cutworms attack young plants, usually right after they are planted out, by cutting through them at the base of the stem. In a polytunnel they are fairly easily avoided if you remember to close your tunnel at night, as the cutworm is the larval stage of the rather drab but widespread turnip moth, which, like most moths, is nocturnal. Unlike most caterpillars, these live in the earth and feed off the roots. Regular cultivation will reveal cutworms, which can then be removed.

Earwigs

Earwigs can be a problem to flower growers, but aren't usually so for vegetable crops. They are fairly easily dealt with by leaving a crumpled piece of cloth on the ground, or a flowerpot stuffed with grass or flannel left upturned on a thin stick in the affected area. Every few days the cloth or pot can be carefully picked up and shaken out in another area of the garden.

Field mice

Field mice will happily take up residence in the shelter a tunnel provides, where they are likely to breed prolifically if given the chance. They cause many different kinds of damage including digging up larger seeds such as peas, beans and squash immediately after planting. If mice are suspected in the tunnel, such sowings should be protected by a propagator lid or cloche until after germination.

Mice invariably make a nuisance of themselves and reproduce extremely quickly, so act promptly if infestation is suspected. A simple mousetrap is usually all that is required, and these can be of the traditional (i.e. fatal) type or the 'humane' sort that trap, but do not kill, the mouse. If you use the latter type of trap, make sure that you are able to check it every few hours during the day as a trapped mouse can dehydrate and die extremely quickly in the heat of a polytunnel in summer. Mice must be released as far away from the tunnel as possible.

A simple mousetrap that you can make yourself is a flat-sided tunnel from the inner tube of a roll of toilet paper. Add a dab of peanut butter to the floor of one end of this, and balance it on the edge of the tunnel staging with a rubbish bin underneath the end with the bait in it (the sides must be at least 50cm (1' 8") high). When the mouse discovers the peanut butter it will tip the tube over and fall into the bin with it, from where you can remove it in the morning.

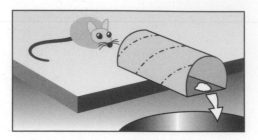

A humane mousetrap

If mice are a persistent problem because of nearby habitat, it may be worth trying the bulbs of an ornamental plant called *Allium moly* (marketed as 'Sork' bulbs), which are said to have a deterrent effect (see the entry on 'Moles' on the opposite page).

Flea beetles

Flea beetles attack early peas and many other crops, especially brassicas. After a few days, the edges of all the leaves look like the perforations on a postage stamp, and while the problem is often cosmetic rather than truly damaging, a severe infestation can seriously diminish a crop. Good housekeeping helps minimize flea beetle infestations. The adults over-winter in plant debris, which should be cleared away from the area around a polytunnel in the autumn. Inside, where the focus might be on year-round crops, clear debris away as it happens.

Horticultural fleece can prevent damage from flea beetle, provided that it is applied at the time of sowing and the plants allowed to grow entirely underneath it. Another common solution is to interplant a tempt-ing sacrificial plant (such as radish) with your food crop. The flea beetles are kept busy eating the radish plants, leaving other growth relatively untouched, and by the time the radishes are removed the seedlings should be large enough to grow away from any damage.

If it is too late for preventative action, one way of reducing flea beetle numbers is to pass a spatula or a piece of card coated with a sticky mate-rial such as lard or treacle over the plants while disturbing them with the other hand. Flea beetles jump when disturbed and so some of them will stick to the grease. This will need to be repeated several times a day for several days. Alternatively, disturbing the host plants so that the flea bee-tles jump away can be followed by quickly covering the plants with fleece, making sure that it is held down to ground level on all sides. As with the sticky trap above, this needs to be done repeatedly over several days.

Leatherjackets

These are crane-fly larvae and feed mainly on grass roots, so they tend to be more of a problem under a well-cared-for lawn than in the veggie patch or polytunnel. However, they will attack lettuce and brassicas, and are even partial to the occasional strawberry. They can also damage young ornamental plants. Although a biocontrol for leatherjackets is marketed under the trade name Nemasys, serious infestation in a polytunnel is unlikely unless it has been newly erected over grass. For normal levels of infestation it should be adequate to cover the affected ground with a black plastic sheet. The grubs will crawl to the surface overnight and can be picked up for relocation the following morning.

Moles

A mole in a polytunnel – especially if you have buried the edges of the cover in a trench – can do a great deal of damage as it tunnels through vegetable root systems in search of earthworms. Trapping is a difficult and specialized job, best undertaken by professionals, but various deterrents are marketed including electronic devices, for which evidence is very scant.

An ornamental plant called *Allium moly* is reputed to repel moles, and bulbs of this plant are sold commercially as mole-repellents under the trade name 'Sork'. It is, however, much less expensive when sold without the brand name. Unsolicited customer reviews vary, but if you have these pests nearby it is probably worth planting some of these around the outside of your tunnel because of the serious consequences should a mole discover the worm-rich beds inside. They should be planted at a distance of no more than 8m (9 yards) apart in a perimeter around the tunnel, and the suppliers of Sork recommend that they be replaced every two years.

A small windmill which alternately lifts and then drops a piece of wood onto the ground or a placed rock will help to deter moles. The sound vibration seems to disturb them, possibly interfering with their ability to listen for prey, and they will go and hunt elsewhere (a similar product is available from Northern Tool in the UK – go to www.northerntooluk.com). While you are trying to persuade a mole to relocate, resist the temptation to disturb runs and molehills. Most of the vandalism perpetrated by moles occurs during the digging out of new tunnels, and once these are established relatively little damage is done.

Onion fly

As with cabbage fly and carrot fly, onion fly is less of a problem in polytunnels than in the open. Onion fly attacks both onion and leeks, and affected bulbs turn yellow and may die. There are no biocontrols available, although interplanting with parsley seems to help, but the most important step to reducing onion fly damage is to grow from set rather than from seed.

Pea moth

The pea moth lays eggs on the pea flower, into which the larva burrows upon hatching. Sometimes only one of the resulting peas is attacked, and sometimes several, but either way a great deal of time and effort is added to harvesting. Covering a vigorous climber like peas with fleece is unlikely to be an option, but since the pea moth is nocturnal it is rarely a visitor to polytunnels provided they are always shut at night. Mesh curtains or screen doors will also help if this pest proves a problem.

Red spider mite

Another pest that can cause serious problems in any covered environment is the red spider mite, which will attack almost anything green. Any incoming plants, especially if donated by well-meaning friends and relatives, should spend a while in your quarantine area until you are sure that they are healthy – but even so, red spider mites are often missed because they are so small, with adults barely visible at 0.5mm (one fiftieth of an inch). The first sign of damage is the development of fine pale mottling developing on the upper surfaces of leaves. Eventually these will turn yellow, and severely affected plants may die. In very heavy infestations a network of very fine webbing may be visible, hence the name (although the mites are actually a yellowish-green colour for most of the year).

Spider mites prefer warm, dry conditions and are therefore more likely to be a problem in greenhouses than polytunnels, the latter being more prone to condensation and higher humidity. However, be alert for early signs of this pest and act quickly. Red spider mites rarely survive for long in the open, so move affected plants outside at the first sign of infection, or nip out affected growth if this is not possible. Spray with a fine mist regularly and often, and the mites will often give up. If not, use a proprietary mite such as *Phytoseiulus persimilis*. It eats spider mites at all stages of life and reproduces roughly twice as fast, but is harmless to plants. It prefers humid conditions.

Sciarid fly (fungus fly)

This is a very common greenhouse and polytunnel pest that damages freshly-planted seedlings in a similar way to cutworms. Plants are nibbled through just below ground level. If only the roots are eaten, plants may be infected with mould – hence the name. The fly affects both container-grown plants and those in beds, and can be found at any time of the year. It prefers warm, damp conditions, and especially likes areas where algae have grown on the surface of the earth – usually a symptom of overwatering. If present, thin and slightly tapering white larvae, roughly 4-6mm long and with tiny black heads, can be found by careful inspection of the top few millimetres of the earth around a prospective planting area. Plants may be covered in small black flies that return quickly when disturbed.

This pest can become serious in the polytunnel environment, and for serious infections in soil beds a biocontrol such as the predatory mite called *Hypoaspis* or the nematode *Steinernema feltiae* is probably the best option. If your area is prone to sciarid fly, then as a preventative measure place grease-coated pieces of yellow card at low level in your tunnel, perhaps attached to seed markers; adult sciarid flies are attracted to the colour yellow, and they will stick to it along with various other flying species.

In containers, sciarid fly can be physically removed by taking out the top 10cm (4") of compost and replacing it. During an infestation, containers can be protected by covering the surface area around the plant with horticultural sand, making it a less inviting area for eggs to be laid, and cutting back on watering as far as possible without stressing the plant.

Slugs and snails

The most serious source of damage to food crops in the garden is probably the humble slug, and to a lesser extent the snail. Both of these are much more likely to attack seedlings and tender young growth than mature plants, except particularly susceptible plants like hostas and lettuces, but there is relatively little that they will not eat. Britain, alas, is the slug capital of the world. Nowhere else does the combination of comparatively warm winters and cool summers – both of which tend to be wet as well – allow such high populations of slugs to survive all year round. But in fact, despite our roughly 30 resident species, we are unlikely to suffer crop damage from more than four of them. That's the good news. The bad news is that those four species are probably the most serious plant predators you will ever find in the garden, and that's why slug pellets are the most commonly used garden pest control in the UK.

The keel slug

If all slugs crawled around on the surface, they would be easier to deal with. However, this species spends most of its time underground – making it primarily a predator of root crops. Because of this preference, getting rid of them without resorting to chemical or biological controls is almost impossible. Otherwise, you can only hope they will not show up in large enough numbers to wipe out an entire crop. Potatoes are their favourite food, and if you suspect an infestation of keel slugs, you should think twice about growing any root crops for a season. Adult keel slugs are quite large at just over 6cm (2⅜") and are dark grey with an orange edge along the keel ridge.

The garden slug

Garden slugs are small, with adults being just over 3cm (1¼") and (usually) black in colour, with a lighter stripe along their sides. Living and feeding underground as well on the surface, they are a serious problem to both root and surface crops. They will feed on just about everything including most seedlings and developing roots.

The field slug

Field slugs are slightly larger than garden slugs and vary between grey and light brown in colour. This slug doesn't burrow, and is a major pest of just about everything that grows above the ground in the garden – including tomatoes.

The black slug

One of our largest slugs, this whopper can grow to around 12.5cm (5"). As its name suggests it's generally black in colour, but other colours have been recorded. Despite its size, it is the least damaging of the four species mentioned here, as its preferred food is decomposing plant matter and manure.

By far the most important factor affecting slug numbers in any environment is their habitat. Slugs are damp creatures and will die if they dry out, so removing plant litter and debris also removes places where they would happily spend the daylight hours before emerging to feed. They also seek shade, so anything they can hide beneath is also a likely hideout. Don't leave empty plant pots, weeds or other debris lying around in the tunnel or surrounding area, as by doing so you will provide just the sort of refuge a slug likes. Keep the soil surface free of clutter of all sorts, and check the bases of any containers regularly. Hoeing the top 5-10 cm (2"-4") of soil has many benefits including the removal of developing weeds, which are another common habitat of sleeping slugs. It has the additional benefit of aerating the soil, helping to incorporate surface applications of compost etc. and preventing the earth from packing into a solid, impervious layer.

Another important factor in slug numbers is predation. In smaller tunnels, providing habitat for slug predators such as ground beetles, frogs and toads may not be practical, but there is still one large predator that will make a huge difference to slug numbers: you.

Andy says:

"Having taken steps to limit slug habitat, adding in a nightly 'slug patrol' armed with a torch and a jam jar is the only slug control measure that I need to take. Done for three or four consecutive evenings each fortnight during warmer weather, slug numbers quickly fall and finding an adult slug in my tunnel is now a rarity."

Mark says:

"Slug patrols here in Wales are absolutely essential – every evening immediately after planting out, and on an 'every other night' basis from early May right up until near the end of June. They even attack the onions and garlic. Without vigilance and copper tape I probably wouldn't have a garden at all."

For blanket control of large areas a species of nematode, *phasmarhabditis hermaphrodita* is used as a biocontrol and is marketed under a variety of names including 'Nemaslug'. Small granules containing the nematodes are dissolved in water and applied to the affected plants. These nematodes are species-specific in that they will not attack other garden wildlife including slug predators. They invade the body of the slug, reproducing inside them and releasing a bacterium that kills them. They then leave their host's body and return to the earth to wait for another slug.

To date, research suggests that using nematodes to control slugs is entirely safe. Once used, however, their numbers drop so drastically that some predator species (such as frogs) are forced to go elsewhere, or starve – in gardening terms, a disaster waiting to happen. In following years the eggs of newly-arrived slugs will have unusually high survival rates, forcing the gardener to apply the biocontrol again and again. However, while this can be a major problem over a large area, when used only in the confined space of a tunnel then, predators should quickly return when the pests reappear.

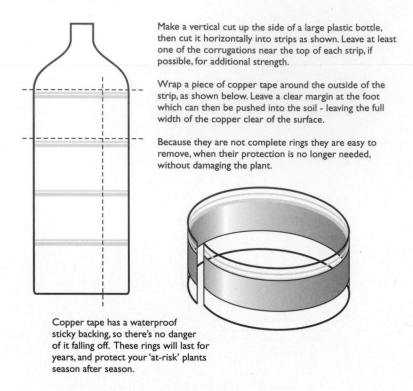

Make a vertical cut up the side of a large plastic bottle, then cut it horizontally into strips as shown. Leave at least one of the corrugations near the top of each strip, if possible, for additional strength.

Wrap a piece of copper tape around the outside of the strip, as shown below. Leave a clear margin at the foot which can then be pushed into the soil - leaving the full width of the copper clear of the surface.

Because they are not complete rings they are easy to remove, when their protection is no longer needed, without damaging the plant.

Copper tape has a waterproof sticky backing, so there's no danger of it falling off. These rings will last for years, and protect your 'at-risk' plants season after season.

Using copper tape to repel slugs

In smaller tunnels it may be more practical to defend particular plants. Although the use of conventional slug pellets can be harmful to wildlife, it is possible to buy pellets based on ferrous phosphate, which is unlikely to cause problems if used sparingly along with slug barriers such as rings cut from plastic drinks bottles. Copper strips around containers and raised beds also act as a barrier to both slugs and snails, as their contact generates a small electric current, which the creatures dislike. Tarnish on the copper reduces the effectiveness – the brighter the metal, the better the protection. Using gravel rather than wood chips as a path surface around raised beds will help to keep them away, and they can also be trapped by partially burying a pot or saucer of liquid in the soil – beer works especially well because the scent attracts them.

Mark says:

> "If the thought of fishing drowned slugs out every morning bothers you, cover the saucer with mesh. The slugs will still be attracted but not drowned, and can be relocated in the morning."

Vine weevil

Weevils aren't usually a serious garden pest in vegetable gardens but can be lethal to container-grown plants of many kinds, including trees, shrubs, and flowers such as cyclamen and begonia. Both larvae and adults attack roots and leaves, causing the plant to wilt and eventually die. The problem can usually be prevented from spreading if a quarantine area is established (see p.84) where newly acquired plants can be left under observation for a while before bringing them into the main garden area.

If you suspect weevil infestation, lift the plants from their pots as soon as possible after purchase and have a good look around to see if either larvae or adults are present. If they are, you could first try replanting in fresh earth after knocking the existing earth from the root ball. Adults can be removed from plants by hand, but have a habit of deliberately dropping to the earth when disturbed, where their dull coloration makes them difficult to find. Be prepared for this by putting a sheet of paper or fleece under the plant before attempting to pick them off.

Vine weevils are relatively inactive during the day, but are much more nimble at night when they feed, so night-time forays with a torch are often frustrating affairs. Traps consisting of a roll of corrugated cardboard may be left for the adults to hide in during the day, and some gardeners have reported success by leaving moist sacking on paths in the evening, returning in the morning to collect and remove the weevils sheltering underneath.

A nematode biocontrol that attacks the larval stage (*Heterohabditis megidis*) is also available. It is usually watered into the earth in spring and again in autumn in order to completely break the weevils' lifecycle.

Whitefly

There are two types of whitefly – those living outside on brassicas, which are known as cabbage whitefly (*Aleyrodes prolabella*), and the greenhouse whitefly (*Trialeurodes vaporariorum*), which only lives in the protection of a greenhouse or polytunnel. Of the two, the greenhouse whitefly is by far the more serious pest. These are found on the underside of leaves as clusters of small white insects which fly up in clouds when disturbed. The damage directly caused by the insects feeding tends to be slight, and a healthy plant can usually withstand it fairly well. Large numbers of whitefly can cause leaves to turn yellow and slow down the growth of the plant. The main source of harm, however, is the sticky honeydew that both adults and larvae (known as 'scales') secrete, which can easily become infected with sooty black moulds, spoiling leaves, fruit and flower-buds.

The first line of defence is healthy soil, encouraging strong vigorous growth that helps plants deal with any pest attack. Second is to ensure a clean environment by removing all plant debris and washing down internal tunnel surfaces during the winter. Eggs of many overwintering pests, including whitefly, will be removed in the process. If a plant becomes infected, whitefly can be washed off with a jet of water, or even vacuumed off the leaves using a dustbuster. Insecticidal soap is another option, but it is only effective if it directly hits the whitefly. If the plant is shaken to encourage the insects to fly, the air can then be sprayed. This is generally more effective than spraying the plant itself. A basic insecticidal soap spray is easily made at home by mixing a tablespoonful of phosphate-free washing-up liquid (such as *Ecover*) and a teaspoonful of vinegar with a litre of water, but do not apply it when the tunnel is very hot. Always test it on a few leaves first, as some plants are easily scorched by soap mixtures.

There are also biocontrols in the form of two species-specific parasitic wasps named *Encarsia Formosa* and *Eretmocerus*. Both lay eggs in whitefly scale. As they are suited to higher temperatures and dry conditions they are not usually employed until the weather becomes warm. There is also a beetle, *Delphastus pusillus*, which eats all stages of whitefly and is used to control severe infestations. However, due to their mobility it is best to confine them by covering the affected plants with fleece prior to introducing the beetles, as otherwise they tend to wander off.

NOTE: It's always a better idea to try non-biological controls first rather than introducing large numbers of predators at the first sign of an infestation.

Woodlice

Woodlice are extremely common and are sometimes a pest, as besides rotting vegetable matter some species are also partial to the roots and stems of young plants and are therefore likely to set up home in your polytunnel. Woodlice tend to congregate in dark, damp places – either under leaf debris, or in the crooks of large plant stems such as on chard or globe artichokes. They are generally nocturnal, and sometimes the only way to distinguish between woodlouse damage and slug damage is to inspect the area for slime trails. Woodlice require damp conditions and cannot survive in dry areas for very long. Their mouthparts are only able to eat soft plant tissue, either because it is very new, or because it has been previously damaged and then further weakened by, for example, a fungal disease.

Unfortunately, mulch often provides an idea habitat for a large concentration of woodlice, which tend to stay in a localized area making them a little easier to deal with. Clear the polytunnel in the spring prior to the main breeding season to cut down on later numbers. Remove any debris on a regular basis, as well as containers, such as pots, and piles of stones.

If you keep pots and other containers in the tunnel, move them regularly to disturb areas where woodlice may breed. Ensure good air circulation by opening the tunnel doors as early as possible, and remove any dead leaves and other debris on a regular basis. Keeping planting clear of the ground is also helpful, so make sure that climbers are trained up wire or trellis rather than allowed to sprawl along the ground. Woodlice are particularly fond of ripening strawberries surrounded by straw, so make sure that the plants are held clear of the ground with supports around fruiting time.

To reduce the numbers of woodlice in your tunnel, leave bait such as cooked potato or a little grated cheese under a tile or plate in a damp area of the tunnel. The woodlice attracted to the site can then be removed the following morning.

* * *

References for Chapter 6

1. US EPA (1987). Integrated Risk Information System p, p'-Dichlorodiphenyltrichloroethane (DDT) (CASRN 50-29-3) __II.A.1. Weight-of-Evidence Characterization.

2. Bouwman H., Sereda B., Meinhardt H.M. (2006). 'Simultaneous presence of DDT and pyrethroid residues in human breast milk from a malaria endemic area in South Africa'. *Environmental Pollution* 144 (3): 902-17.

3. USDA, Pesticide Data Program Annual Summary Calendar Year 2005, November 2006.

4. Dr Bill Symondson, Cardiff School of Biosciences, *The New 'Gardeners' World' Handbook*, 1990, BBC Books.

5. Williams G.M., Kroes R., Munro I.C. (2000). 'Safety evaluation and risk assessment of the herbicide Roundup and its active ingredient, glyphosate, for humans'. *Regulatory Toxicology and Pharmacology* 31 (2): 117-165.

6. Fernandeza M.R., Sellesa F., Gehlb D., DePauwa R.M. and Zentner R.P. 'Crop Ecology, Management & Quality', published online August 26th 2005.

7. See www.monsanto.com/investors/financial_reports.

8. Source: Agence France Presse, Jan 26, 2007 reported in www.organicconsumers.org/articles/article_4114.cfm.

Chapter 7

Thinking Outside the Tunnel

Alternative uses for your structure

Thus far this book has dealt mainly with growing vegetables. This is by far the most popular use for polytunnels, but not the only use – tunnel structures are extremely versatile, and their applications extremely varied.

Leisure

Although polytunnels are sometimes used solely to cover areas for leisure use, such as swimming pools, it is far more common to see part of a tunnel being given over to living space, enhanced by the business of growing carrying on around it. Seating areas and hammocks, hung from the crop bars, are particularly popular. These are best situated at one end so that occupants can take advantage of any breeze in sunny weather – if you are still at the planning stage, do not underestimate how warm tunnels can get when the sun shines. Situating a small patio in a tunnel is also quite possible, planning permitting, and some Mediterranean planting such as a (dwarf) lemon tree can turn these into really special places. Since everything is actually growing, there is none of the artificial atmosphere that such areas have when they are set up in office buildings and shopping centres.

Hot tubs are another popular addition in larger tunnels, but beware. Pat Bowcock at Ourganics in Dorset had to remove her tub, heated by coppiced willow in a woodburner; not because of fumes or heat, but because it was so popular that its use interfered with her watering schedule. Not so the solar shower, which is happily still there.

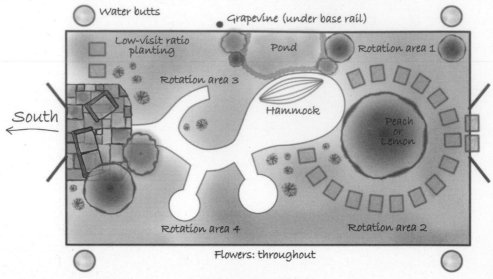

Fantasy tunnel layout

Livestock

Another popular use for tunnels is to provide a more sheltered environment for animals in winter. Most livestock can cope with very low temperatures without any problem, but long spells of wet weather can take their toll unless some protection is offered. Animals that are able to retreat to a dry, sheltered environment during cold weather consume less feed, suffer fewer illnesses (and have lower vet's bills) and are generally happier all round.

Chickens are the most common animal to be housed in a domestic tunnel, since they are undemanding and can be kept in even the smallest garden. Although they could be completely confined to the tunnel for the whole winter provided it is well ventilated, chickens much prefer to have access to grass and the bugs in it – and nutritional analysis has shown that they need these components in their diet in order to develop high levels of health-giving omega-3 fatty acids in their dark meat, an important consideration if you are planning to eat any birds. If the chickens have a grassy area close by, it can be linked to the tunnel for the winter using tread-in fence posts, and the birds given access to it during the day. The whole tunnel can be turned over to the birds provided there are no crops to consume, or you can create a partition to (hopefully) keep them away from your food crops. This arrangement also works well for other livestock, albeit on a different scale.

When keeping any livestock in a polythene-skinned tunnel, the cover has to be protected from the animals in some fashion. Professionals use purpose-built tunnels with wooden sides, which can be replaced by mesh in the summer. This is not practical for a home-scale operation, so one good solution is to arrange bales of straw around the edge of the tunnel to prevent the animals from coming into contact with the cover. There are a hundred and one uses for straw in any organic garden, including its use as a compost ingredient, so the bales will not be wasted.

Once again, please note that polytunnels are not suitable for livestock during the summer because they get too hot. If you wish to provide year-round protection for animals, opt for a model with a side rail; fit polythene on the top section and shade netting on the sides.

One use for spare straw bales in the tunnel is to ease the watering requirements for container-grown tomato plants. Three weeks before planting out is due, cut holes just big enough to take the pots to half of their depth into the top of the straw bales, two pots per bale. You will need an extremely sharp knife for this, and we suggest doing it well away from the cover. Remove the pots again, and saturate the bales with water. Keep them just wet for the next three weeks (this time is necessary because the straw tends to heat up initially), and pull any grass sprouts out of the bale as they appear. Once the plants are up to their full pot size, put a couple of handfuls of compost into the bottom of each planting hole and cut the bottom off the pots, then push them firmly into the holes. Once the plants root into the straw they will be unlikely to dry out, and can be left for several days between waterings if needs be.

Innovations

One of the beauties of polytunnels is that they are unashamedly low-tech; a tunnel is, after all, only an overgrown cloche with ideas above its station. This lends the structure to all sorts of adaptations and Heath-Robinson tinkering, as we soon found out in our research. Water-barrel heat sinks enhanced with solar heaters, guinea pig manure for fertility, yoghurt-making and bread-proving (a great example of lateral thinking, and a very tasty lunch), tunnels butted up to the kitchen door . . . the applications of polytunnels are as varied as the people who own them.

A slug-free suspended shelf can be created by hanging a plank from the crop bars – a good argument for having them – and if a wider platform is used this can become suspended staging. Such an arrangement needs a support at each corner to minimise rocking, and this can be provided by fitting four separate attachment points or by cradling the end of the plank in a loop, the ends of which are tied to each of the crop bar's diagonal struts.

Being nearer the ridge-pole where warm air becomes trapped, such a shelf tends to be a little warmer than the rest of the tunnel. If you are particularly passionate about strawberries and extremely keen to have them early, you can take advantage of this heat and put growbags on your shelf, or create a 'suspended gutter' by fixing lengths of 5cm x 10cm (2"x 4") timber on each edge of it. This gutter can be lined with a single offcut of polythene cover and hung at neck height, with one end raised a little higher than the other. The guttering is then filled with compost and planted up with strawberries (or other suitable plants such as chilli peppers).

Strawberry Gutter

The gutter is left open at the lower end, from which a tin can may be hung or placed on the soil below. This is so that the gutter can be watered entirely from its high end, applying the water slowly from a hose or dripper bottle, or at intervals from a can. As the compost soaks through, the water trickles along the length of the gutter and when you hear drips falling into the tin can it is time to stop watering. Strawberries grown this way can be mulched without fear of slugs or crawling insects sheltering under it.

Inside the tunnel, regular (June-bearing) strawberries will fruit during May – and a few such plants can be a useful way to stretch the season. However, a more effective way to use strawberries is to choose a day-neutral variety, which will keep fruiting until temperatures really drop in the winter. For the best yields, remove all flowers as they form until the latter half of June, so that the plant concentrates its energy on root and leaf production. Plants grown in this way should be treated as annuals, and composted at the end of fruiting; after this, the gutter shelf can be flipped over to its plain side and used as a suspended shelf until next year.

Cucumbers, melons and other curcubits are a common feature in polytunnels, but with fewer attachment points available than in a greenhouse, supporting the plants can be problematic. To avoid potentially nasty encounters between bamboo canes and the tunnel cover, plants can be grown up lengths of synthetic twine or coated wire (natural twine is not suitable for the method described below, as it rots quickly in tunnel conditions). Begin by tying a length of thick wire to run horizontally along the tunnel above head height, using the crop bars or the tops of the cross-braces. The plants will grow towards this wire, and it does not have to be directly above the planting area; the plants will be happy at any angle, so you can lean them in from both sides of a path or away from shade-hating plants as you wish.

At the time of planting out pot-raised seedlings, tie a piece of synthetic twine to the wire, and leave the twine ball on the ground. Working downwards from the top, tie off short loops every 15cm (6") or so until you reach the planting station, and allow an extra 25cm (10") before cutting the twine. Dig the planting hole, and tie a wide loop in the spare twine so that it will lie just at the bottom of the planting hole. Knock the plant out of its pot, put the root ball firmly on top of the twine, and plant and water in as normal. As the roots grow they will anchor the twine loop to the ground, providing a firm attachment.

Wrap the plants gently around the twine as they grow, using the loops as attachment points. This system works well for any tall plants needing support, including curcubits, beans and tomatoes, but for plants such as melons with large, heavy fruits, it may be beneficial to provide additional horizontal supports. This can be done by running additional twine or short lengths of cane between the loops of neighbouring planting stations. This is tricky to do once the plants are in full growth, so it is best set up at planting time.

Exotics

Chilli peppers, grape vines and aubergines are one thing, but some growers take things a step further. With a little know-how, a polytunnel gives you the opportunity to grow quite a variety of exotic fruits, vegetables and other plants. Trying new things – and sometimes quite unlikely things – is part of what makes gardening such a stimulating activity.

Polytunnels are suitable for a wide variety of exotic plants, many of which will overwinter successfully without the provision of any additional heat. These can include guavas and lowquats, key limes, nectarines and peaches, a wider variety of figs than outdoors, olives, grapes, dragon fruits, pomegranates and feijoa, a native of Brazil. Growing citrus fruits including grapefruit, oranges, lemons and limes is also possible, but these should not be subjected to temperatures below 5°C, so a double-insulated enclosure and possibly some supplementary heat will be necessary except in the mildest of microclimates.

When dealing with exotics it is easy to overlook the smaller plants. Lemongrass does well within the confines of a tunnel, and can be propagated easily from stock bought from Asian supermarkets. If stood in a jar of water, a stalk of lemongrass will develop roots within two or three weeks, and can then be potted up or planted out in the beds where it will grow as a perennial, and should be cut back hard every autumn. Home-grown lemongrass has a much more intense, lemony flavour than shop-bought produce, which is often rather tired after its journey.

Shop-bought ginger and turmeric roots will also take very easily; choose roots that are showing fat yellow buds, and cut the bud section off with at least 5cm of root. Bury the root, bud facing upwards, an inch deep in a large pot of compost or directly into the soil bed, give some shade, and do not allow it to dry out. If container-grown, ginger needs to be fed every two or three weeks with a general purpose feed. Low light levels in the winter make ginger hard to overwinter, but if water is restricted in the autumn it will give you a fine crop of rhizomes just as the cold weather closes in.

Following some pioneering work at the Tregothnan estate near Truro in Cornwall, it is now possible to buy genuine tea plants (*Camellia sinensis*) which have been grown here in the UK, although the plant is so acid-loving (pH 4.5-6.5) that in most locations it would do best in a pot (no, not a teapot – that comes later). Tea needs lots of moisture and top-dressing with well-rotted manure, and is sensitive to sun-scorch. If you find that this is a problem even with the diffusion effect of the polythene film, then a small section of 40% shade net may need to be draped over the plant during the summer. Tea is easy to propagate by taking cuttings, a few inches long with a heel, in the autumn. You might remember that cup of tea that we urged you to have before you secure and tighten your tunnel cover, in *Self-build Tunnels* p.41 – but by the time you have to re-cover your tunnel, you could be making it with leaves from your very own plants.

* * *

Afterword

Over the course of this book, we have tried to write the 'how-to' manual that we would have liked to have been given when we started out with our own tunnels. Polytunnel users are an inventive and varied bunch, but during the course of our research we saw the same set of very basic questions being asked on internet forums time and time again. It was clear that people were having to muddle through with very little information. We hope that this book will help.

In particular, we hope that the information here will encourage a few people to take a few steps towards becoming more self-sufficient. There is gathering evidence that the age of cheap energy is coming to a close, and anything that you can do to reduce your dependence on the chain of food distribution can only be a good thing. So get growing: note your planting and harvesting dates year-to-year, always be ready to try something new – and good luck from both of us.

Further Information and Suppliers

Websites

www.farminmypocket.co.uk Our own website, featuring more information on polytunnel use, gardening and homesteading tips, and straightforward how-to guides. Also features our blog, so you can see what we're sowing, growing and harvesting week by week.

www.selfsufficientish.com A very busy community website. Although self-sufficientish does not have a specific polytunnel forum, there is never any shortage of help on hand. An invaluable resource for anyone wishing to become more self-reliant.

www.polytunnels.tv Shows footage of the different stages of building a polytunnel.

http://sallygardens.freeforums.org Run by Rebecca and Dan Hillman, the Sallygardens website charts the setting-up and evolution of an organic smallholding. Rebecca and Dan have found their polytunnel so important that they have allocated a forum to it.

www.gardeningtalk.com and **www.vegetable-gardens.co.uk** General gardening sites which regularly feature polytunnel threads.

http://groups.yahoo.com/group/polytunnels-chat Ask questions of other members in the classic yahoo! group format.

Manufacturers and Retailers, Great Britain

Citadel
32 St Andrews Crescent
Stratford-upon-Avon
Warwickshire CV37 9QL
01789 297456
www.citadelpolytunnels.com

CLM Keder Greenhouses
Newtown
Offenham
Evesham, Worcestershire
WR11 8RZ
01386 49094
www.kedergreenhouse.co.uk

Clovis Lande Associates Ltd
Branbridges Road
East Peckham
Tonbridge
Kent TN12 5HH
01622 873900
www.polytunnels.com

Fargro Ltd (covers only)
Toddington Lane
Littlehampton
West Sussex BN17 7PP
01903 726100
www.fargro.co.uk

Ferryman Polytunnels Ltd
Bridge Road
Lapford
Crediton
Devon EX17 6AE
01363 83444
www.ferryman.uk.com

First Tunnels Ltd
Dixon Street
Barrowford
Lancashire
BB9 8PL
01282 601253
www.firsttunnels.co.uk

Five Star Polytunnels
Unit 2, Cellan
Lampeter
Ceredigion
SA48 8HU
01570 421580
www.polytunnels.me.uk

Greenhouses UK.com
Millpool
Bodmin
Cornwall PL30 4HY
01208 821350 (or 0845 6449394
within the UK)
www.greenhouses-uk.com

Haygrove Ltd
Redbank
Ledbury
Herefordshire HR8 2JL
01531 633659
www.haygrove.co.uk

Highland Polytunnels
Romany House
Easterton
Dalcross, Inverness IV2 7JE
01667 462209
www.highlandpolytunnels.co.uk

Manufacturers and Retailers, Great Britain (continued)

Knowle Nets Ltd
East Road, Bridport,
Dorset DT6 4NX
01308 424342
www.knowlenets.co.uk

McGregor Polytunnels Ltd
Winton Farm
Petersfield Road
Ropley
Hampshire SO24 0HB
01962 772368
www.mcgregorpolytunnels.co.uk

National Polytunnels
4 Cable Court
Pittman Way
Fulwood
Preston
Lancashire PR2 9YW
01772 799200
www.nationalpolytunnels.co.uk

Northern Polytunnels
Mill Green
Waterside Road
Colne
Lancashire BB8 0TA
01282 873120
www.northernpolytunnels.co.uk

Polybuild Ltd
Upper Chancton Farm
London Road
Washington
West Sussex RH20 3DH
01903 892333
www.polybuild.com

Polyhouses.com
A division of Fordingbridge plc
Arundel Road
Fontwell
Arundel
West Sussex BN18 0SD
01243 554455
www.polyhouses.com

Polythene One.Com
(covers specialists only)
152 Marshside Road
Marshside
Southport
Merseyside PR9 9SY
01704 505875
www.polytheneone.com

Polytunnelsonline.com
Bonehill Farm
Tamworth
Staffs B78 3HP
www.polytunnelsonline.com

Solar Tunnels Ltd
Unit 2, Cottons Yard
Storrington
West Sussex RH20 3EA
01903 742615
www.solartunnels.co.uk

Two Wests & Elliott Ltd
Unit 4 Carrwood Road
Sheepbridge Industrial Estate
Chesterfield
Derbyshire S41 9RH
01246 451077
www.twowests.co.uk

Manufacturers and Retailers, Northern Ireland & Republic of Ireland

Colm Warren Polyhouses Ltd
Kilmurray
Trim
County Meath, Eire
+353 (0) 469 546007
www.cwp.ie

J. F. McKenna Ltd
66 Cathedral Road
Armagh
County Armagh
Northern Ireland BT61 8AE
028 375 24800
www.jfmckenna.com

Morris Polythene Greenhouses Ltd
53a Lenagh Road
Drumlea
Omagh, County Tyrone
Northern Ireland BT79 7RG
028 8164 8205
www.morrispolytunnels.co.uk

**National Agrochemical
Distributors** (covers and sundries)
Blake's Cross
Lusk, County Dublin, Eire
+353 (1) 8437808
www.nad.ie

Further Reading

Four-Season Harvest: Organic Vegetables from Your Home Garden All Year Long (revised edition), Eliot Coleman, Chelsea Green Publishing Company, 1999. A broader look at the issues of growing under cover in an area with extremely cold winters.

The New Create an Oasis With Greywater: Choosing, Building and Using Greywater Systems, Art Ludwig, Oasis Design, 2006. In its 5th edition, this book is essential reading for anyone intending to reuse greywater.

Organic Gardening: The Natural No-dig Way, Charles Dowding, Green Books 2007. An extremely useful book because the author uses no pesticides and concentrates on the condition of his soil.

Permaculture Two: Practical Design for Town and Country in Permanent Agriculture, Bill Mollison, Tagari Publications, 1979. Mollison's books started the whole Permaculture movement off, and this is still worth reading for a broad understanding of the concepts involved.

Planning the Organic Vegetable Garden, Dick Kitto, Thorsons, 1986. If you're into hardcore planning, Dick Kitto's book provides a technical but cast-iron tool for making sure not a scrap of ground is wasted.

Glossary

Actinomycetes: A group of soil bacteria playing an important role in decomposition of organic materials such as cellulose and chitin, essential for humus formation.

Airflow house: See shade house.

Anchor bolt: An accessory specific to solar tunnels, anchor bolts are screwed into the soil to anchor the structure in place, and can be removed by turning in the opposite direction.

Anchor plate: An accessory that is fixed to the bottom of ground tubes and covered with soil. An effective alternative to concreting in.

Anti-hotspot tape: Cover-safe, padded adhesive tape which is used to cushion the cover against the abrasive effects of the metal frame.

Base plate: An alternative to ground tubes when erecting a tunnel on a hard surface.

Base rail: A horizontal metal or wooden rail or purlin to which the edge of the cover may be fixed as an alternative to burying it in a trench.

Biocontrol: Pest control using the deliberate introduction of predatory or disease organisms.

Brace: A support strut. Diagonal braces are used to make tunnel frames more rigid.

BTU: British Thermal Unit. A unit of energy, used here to describe heat output.

Builders' band: A perforated, flexible metal band which can be used to suspend pipework. Known as 'plumbers' tape' in the US.

Capillary bed: A flat expanse of capillary matting, which can draw water from an attached reservoir and thus remain wet. Containers and trays may be left on the capillary bed and will not dry out so long as the reservoir is not allowed to run dry.

Climate zone: See Hardiness zone.

Cloche: A protective structure creating a bubble of still air to shield plants, typically against wind or low temperatures. Cloches can be constructed of plastic or glass, or made of a variety of films and fabrics suspended over the plants with a frame.

Cold frame: A transparent-roofed enclosure, built low to the ground to protect plants from cold weather.

Crop bar: A metal tube fixed across the hoops above head height. Crop bars confer additional structural strength, and can be used as strong attachment points for a variety of applications. Known as trusses in the US.

Crop rotation: The practice of growing different crop groups in succession to avoid the build-up of soil pests, and to avoid excessive depletion of the soil.

Double-digging: A gardening technique for the deep cultivation of soil in two layers, and the incorporation of organic matter.

Drip hose: Perforated or porous hose used to deliver water slowly along its whole length, often used under a surface mulch, or just under the soil surface.

Fleece: A extremely lightweight row-cover fabric, which retains ground heat and offers protection from insects. Known as 'floating row cover' in the US.

Greenhouse effect: The process by which a light-transparent structure traps heat, becoming warmer than the surrounding air.

Greywater: Water previously used for bathing, washing or laundry, but excluding toilet waste. Known as 'graywater' in the US.

Ground tubes: Steel tubes or posts hammered into the ground, onto which assembled hoops are pushed.

Hardiness zone: A geographically-defined zone in which a specific group of plants will grow, as defined by their ability to withstand the minimum temperatures of the zone.

Hoop: The curved support that gives a polytunnel its distinctive shape. Generally used to mean a complete assembly, from ground tube to apex. Can also be in the shape of a gothic arch, particularly in the US where it is used because of its superior ability to shed snow.

Horticultural fleece: See Fleece.

Hotspot tape, hot-spot tape: Synonyms for anti-hotspot tape.

Nematode: Microscopic roundworms, parasitic forms of which are commonly used as biocontrols for a variety of garden pests.

Opacifiers: Chemicals added to polytunnel film to scatter incoming light, reducing scorch and diffusing shadows to reduce shading.

Organic: Organic farming is a form of agriculture that excludes the use of synthetic fertilizers, herbicides and pesticides, and genetically modified organisms. There is some evidence that organic produce is more nutritious than conventionally-produced food, and pesticide contamination is substantially lower.

Permaculture: A design ethos which views a garden (or any other system) as a holistic structure made up of interrelated parts, which also interacts with the wider environment.

Raised bed: A growing area, with or without a supporting frame, in which the growing medium is deliberately higher than the surrounding area.

Ridge-pole: A rigid pipe forming the centre purlin or 'spine' of a tunnel frame.

Sacrificial plant: a plant used specifically to attract pests to a particular area, decoying them away from crops.

Shade tunnel: A tunnel frame covered by shade fabric, rather than by polythene film.

Side rail: Similar to a base rail, but fixed at a higher level to allow the lower portion of the hoops to be covered with a different material than the upper portion.

Soak hose: A synonym for drip hose.

Soil bed: An area of flat ground used and maintained for plant-growing.

Staging: A generic term for any flat surface used as a bench in a tunnel or greenhouse. Staging can be a solid surface or wire mesh, and is used as a workspace and for setting out containers. Commercial staging is often too low for comfortable work, because it is designed for small greenhouses with poor headroom.

Storm braces: Short lengths of pipe clamped over the intermediate joints on tunnel hoops, to confer additional joint strength in exposed locations.

Trenched installation: A tunnel for which no base rail has been used, the cover instead being buried in a trench. This method of fixing the cover in place is inexpensive but hard work, and care must be taken that the frame design allows tightening of the cover once the trench has been backfilled.

UV-stabilised: Containing additives that prevent ultraviolet light from weakening the plastic. Unstabilised plastic usually only lasts for one season before becoming brittle.

Zones, Permaculture: A way of anticipating, and planning for, the amount of human activity an area needs. These can be thought of as a series of concentric rings with zone 0, the dwelling itself, in the centre. A polytunnel is categorized as zone 1, needing frequent visits.

Index

ORGANIC GARDENING
The natural no-dig way

Charles Dowding

*"One of our most respected vegetable growers . . .
Now ordinary gardeners can benefit from his years
of practical experience, growing great vegetables in
harmony with Mother Earth." –* Joy Larkcom

*"Charles is a passionate and accomplished gardener who
grows vegetables of amazing flavour."*
– Raymond Blanc

ISBN 978 1 903998 91 5 £10.95 paperback

SALAD LEAVES
FOR ALL SEASONS
Organic growing from pot to plot

Charles Dowding

"An essential book for every garden and kitchen"
–Nigel Slater

Here is all the information you need for productive,
healthy and tasty salads. Learn the subtleties of salad
seasons, and the virtues of growing different leaves throughout the year. And
when your table is groaning with the abundance of your harvests, there are deli-
cious and imaginative recipes from Susie, Charles' wife, exploiting the fantastic
flavours, colour and vitality of home-grown salad leaves.

ISBN 978 1 900322 20 1 £10.95 paperback

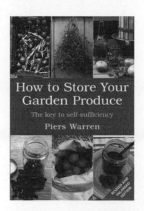

HOW TO STORE YOUR GARDEN PRODUCE
The key to self-sufficiency

Piers Warren

With less than an acre of garden you can grow enough produce to feed a family of four for a year, but as much of the produce will ripen simultaneously in the summer, without proper storage most of it will go to waste and you'll be off to the supermarket again. Learn simple and enjoyable techniques for storing your produce and embrace the wonderful world of self-sufficiency.

In the A-Z list of produce, each entry includes recommended varieties, suggested methods of storage and a number of recipes.

ISBN 978 1 900322 17 1 £7.95 paperback

SURVIVING AND THRIVING ON THE LAND
How to use your time and energy to run a successful smallholding

Rebecca Laughton

It's a dream come true when you finally get a piece of land or join an eco-community, and start to plan your sustainable land-based enterprise. But all too often the dream is spoiled by lack of money, stress, exhaustion and poor time management, and your work and future plans can dissolve into discord, illness and poverty. Smallholdings provide food, home, fuel and employment for those who run them, and local, seasonal, often organic and ethical food and timber for an expanding market.

Surviving and Thriving on the Land looks at ways in which projects can be designed that care for the people involved in them as well as the earth that they are trying to protect. This book offers a framework, backed up by real life examples, of issues to consider when setting up a new project, or for overcoming human-energy-based problems in existing projects.

ISBN 978 1 900322 28 7 £12.95 paperback

ALLOTMENT GARDENING
An organic guide for beginners

Susan Berger

"Clear, down to earth and inspiring, this is a manual
for serious gardeners in the making."
– *Organic Gardening*

This practical guide is aimed at those who have not had
an allotment before, or are new to growing their own,
it's packed with advice – from choosing and planning your allotment through to
harvesting and storing your produce. Part One covers tools, planning and clearing the site, soil types, crop rotation, planting and protecting plants, design,
growing techniques, common problems, and a gardener's calendar. Part Two
includes an A–Z of vegetables, fruits, herbs and flowers, companion planting,
storage tips, and a directory of seed suppliers and useful organisations.

ISBN 978 1 903998 54 0   £9.95 paperback

FOREST GARDENING
Rediscovering nature and community
in a post-industrial age

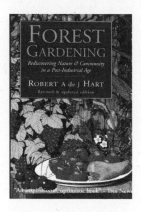

Robert A. de J. Hart

This is Robert Hart's classic manual about the principles
of forest gardening. Designed to achieve the utmost
economy of space and labour, a forest garden is a tiny
imitation of a natural forest. Once established, it requires minimal maintenance,
and can provide year-round produce of herbs, fruit and nuts, and root and perennial vegetables. Includes guidelines on how to design and maintain a forest gardens, and lists of recommended species for temperate, tropical and sub-tropical
climates.

ISBN 978 1 900322 02 7   £10.95 paperback

For our complete booklist, see www.greenbooks.co.uk